AZTECS:
REIGN OF BLOOD
& SPLENDOR

Time-Life Books is a division of Time Life
Inc., a wholly owned subsidiary of
THE TIME INC. BOOK COMPANY

TIME-LIFE BOOKS

PRESIDENT: Mary N. Davis

MANAGING EDITOR: Thomas H. Flaherty
Director of Editorial Resources: Elise D. Ritter-
  Clough
Executive Art Director: Ellen Robling
Director of Photography and Research: John
  Conrad Weiser
Editorial Board: Dale M. Brown, Janet Cave,
  Roberta Conlan, Laura Foreman, Jim Hicks,
  Blaine Marshall, Rita Thievon Mullin,
  Henry Woodhead
*Assistant Director of Editorial Resources/Training
  Manager:* Norma E. Shaw

PUBLISHER: Robert H. Smith

Associate Publisher: Sandra Lafe Smith
Editorial Director: Russell B. Adams, Jr.
Marketing Director: Anne C. Everhart
Director of Production Services: Robert N. Carr
Production Manager: Prudence G. Harris
Supervisor of Quality Control: James King

Editorial Operations
Production: Celia Beattie
Library: Louise D. Forstall
Computer Composition: Deborah G. Tait
  (Manager), Monika D. Thayer, Janet
  Barnes Syring, Lillian Daniels
Interactive Media Specialist: Patti H. Cass

**Library of Congress
Cataloging in Publication Data**
Aztecs: Reign of blood & splendor / by the
editors of Time-Life Books.
    p. cm.—(Lost civilizations)
  Includes bibliographical references and index.
  ISBN 0-8094-9854-5 (trade)
  ISBN 0-8094-9855-3 (lib. bdg.)
    1. Aztecs.   I. Time-Life Books. II. Series.
F1219.73.A975   1992
972'.018—dc20   91-40751

LOST CIVILIZATIONS

SERIES EDITOR: Dale M. Brown
Series Administrators: Norma E. Shaw,
  Philip Brandt George

Editorial staff for: *Aztecs: Reign of Blood &
  Splendor*
Art Director: Barbara M. Sheppard
Picture Editor: Tina McDowell
Text Editors: Charlotte Anker, Kenneth C.
  Danforth, Robert Somerville
Associate Editors/Research: Patricia Mitchell,
  Jacqueline L. Shaffer
Assistant Art Director: Bill McKenney
Writer: Darcie Conner Johnston
Senior Copy Coordinator: Anne Farr
Picture Coordinator: Gail Feinberg
Editorial Assistant: Patricia D. Whiteford

Special Contributors: Tony Allan, George
Constable, Ellen Galford, Lydia Preston
Hicks, Gina Maranto, Robert Menaker, Roy
Reed, Griffin Smith, Jr., Daniel Stashower,
Bryce Walker (text); Vilasini Balakrishnan,
Paul Edholm, Ira Gitlin, Jocelyn G. Lindsay,
Mary Grace Mayberry, Vickie Morrison,
Susan Perry, Gail Prensky, Sumathi Raghavan,
Johanna J. Ramos, Eugenia S. Scharf, Bonnie
Stutski (research); Roy Nanovic (index)

Correspondents: Elisabeth Kraemer-Singh
(Bonn), Christine Hinze (London), Patricia
Alisau, Christina Lieberman (New York),
Maria Vincenza Aloisi (Paris), Ann Natanson
(Rome). Valuable assistance was also provided
by: Trini Bandrés, Pilar Gore (Madrid);
Andrea Dabrowski (Mexico City); Elizabeth
Brown (New York); Leonora Dodsworth,
Ann Wise (Rome).

The Consultants:
H. B. Nicholson, professor of anthropology at
the University of California, Los Angeles, has
studied the ancient peoples of Mesoamerica
for almost 40 years.

John B. Carlson, director of the Center for
Archaeoastronomy in College Park, Maryland,
has viewed every important Aztec site through
the lens of astronomy.

Richard A. Diehl, chairman of the anthropology department at the University of Alabama,
has excavated extensively at Olmec and Toltec
sites and at the ancient and monumental city
of Teotihuacan.

Davíd Carrasco directs the Mesoamerican Archive and Research Project at the University
of Colorado. His research focuses on Aztec
ceremonial centers.

George L. Cowgill, professor of anthropology
at Arizona State University, has directed archaeological fieldwork at Teotihuacan and
other sites in Mexico.

*For information on and a full description of any of the
Time-Life Books series listed above, please call 1-800-621-
7026 or write:*
Reader Information
Time-Life Customer Service
P.O. Box C-32068
Richmond, Virginia 23261-2068

This volume is one in a series that explores the
worlds of the past, using the finds of archaeologists
and other scientists to bring ancient peoples and
their cultures vividly to life.

GULF OF MEXICO

PACIFIC OCEAN

Lake Tetzcoco

AZTEC EMPIRE

N

SIERRA MADRE ORIENTAL

ROUTE OF CORTÉS

Cempoala

Veracruz

Pico de Orizaba

OLMEC HEAD

AZTECS:
REIGN OF BLOOD
& SPLENDOR

By the Editors of Time-Life Books
TIME-LIFE BOOKS, ALEXANDRIA, VIRGINIA

CONTENTS

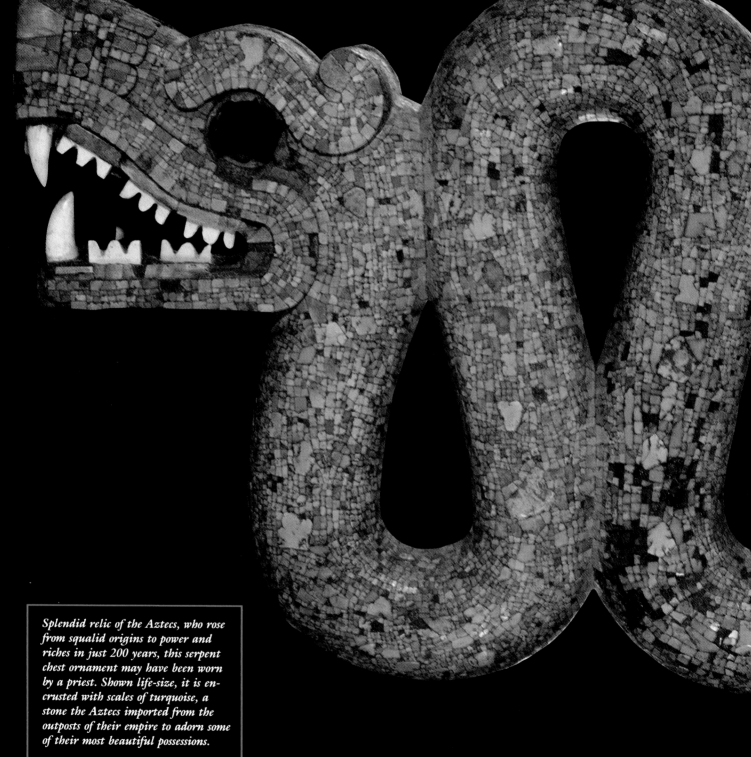

Splendid relic of the Aztecs, who rose from squalid origins to power and riches in just 200 years, this serpent chest ornament may have been worn by a priest. Shown life-size, it is encrusted with scales of turquoise, a stone the Aztecs imported from the outposts of their empire to adorn some of their most beautiful possessions.

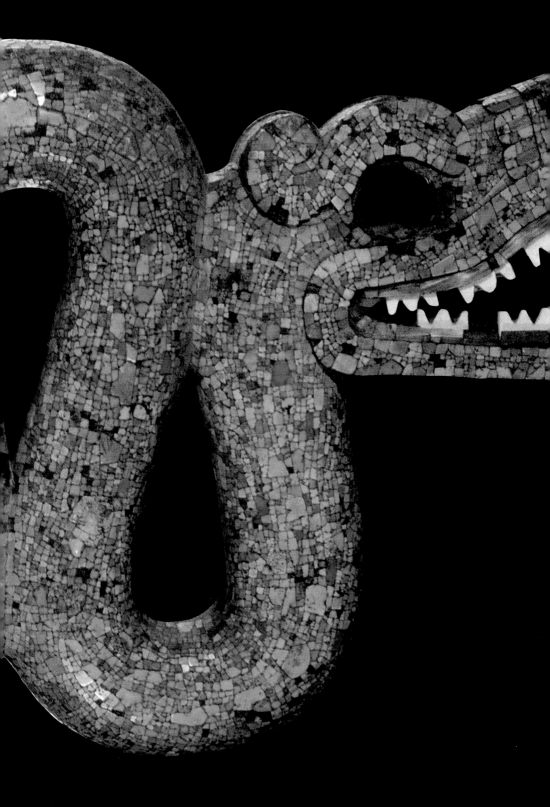

THE FALL OF
THE CITY
"PRECIOUS AS JADE"

The tough old Spanish soldier remembered that day in 1519 when he first saw the private gardens of Motecuhzoma, the Aztec ruler. "We went to the orchard and garden, which was a marvelous place both to see and to walk in," wrote Bernal Díaz del Castillo, a much-scarred veteran of Hernán Cortés's campaign to conquer Mexico. "I never tired of noticing the diversity of trees and the various scents given off by each, and the paths choked with roses and other flowers, and the many local fruit trees and the pond of fresh water. Everything was shining and decorated with different kinds of stonework and paintings that were a marvel to gaze on. Then there were birds of many breeds and varieties that came to the pond."

Out of nostalgia, Díaz began to reflect on the fate of Aztec Mexico. "I thought that no land like it would ever be discovered in the whole world," he recalled wistfully. "But today all that I then saw is overthrown and destroyed; nothing is left standing."

Four decades after the arrival of the Spaniards the conquest of the empire of the Aztecs was complete. The worship of fierce gods had begun to pass from living memory, and now the descendants of Aztec warriors—Spanish subjects all—worshiped Jesus Christ. A new city had grown atop the ruins of their temples.

In 1790, almost three centuries after Díaz first beheld the

Rattlesnakes form a skirt for this 12-ton statue of the decapitated Aztec earth mother, Coatlicue, dug up in 1790 in Mexico City. From the stem of her neck, blood gushes forth in the shape of two additional serpents.

wonders of Tenochtitlan, the resplendent Aztec capital, the Spanish viceroy in Mexico City ordered some paving and the construction of a drainage system. In the broad expanse of a square known as the Zócalo, the glare of the late summer sun threw a dusty jumble of trenches into sharp relief. Along the southeastern side of the plaza, in the shadows of the National Palace, a team of workmen wielded shovels. Occasionally one or another of them would pause to wipe his sweat-beaded brow or gaze across the square at the baroque cathedral. It was to spare the cathedral, the palace, and the square itself from periodic flooding that this project had been ordered.

Amid the desultory chatter of the workmen, a sound of metal hitting stone rang out, and soon the crew had gathered around a single spot. The trenching had struck a sizable impediment, and a flurry of shovels attacked the obstacle. As the dirt flew, the men's pulses quickened, for the object emerging from the shrouding layers of earth was an enormous figure unlike any they had ever seen before. Powerful and vaguely human in form, the figure was enrobed in a skirt of woven serpents. When fully exhumed, it proved to be an impressive eight feet five inches long. Lying in the soil in grotesque repose, it had claws for feet and hands and bore what looked like a face composed of two rearing, fanged snake heads, set threateningly nose to nose. Most disturbing was the adornment that hung across the figure's breast, a necklace strung with lifelike human hands and hearts ranged around a clench-jawed human skull.

The news that a relic of the long-buried Aztec religion had been dug up at the very core of the metropolis took 18th-century Mexico—and later the wider world— by surprise. Europeans in particular had not realized that the Aztecs had had the technical skill required to transport and handle such

ROAD MAP TO THE END OF THE WORLD

One of the most imposing—and significant—of Aztec relics is the intricately carved circular stone seen below. It is 4 feet thick, 12 feet in diameter, and weighs more than 24 tons. Because symbols for the days of the 20-day Aztec calendar encircle it, the disk came to be called the Calendar Stone shortly after its discovery in 1790 beneath Mexico City's central square.

Today, however, scholars recognize that the stone was no mere calendar. The glyphs and icons adorning it were a road map of the Aztecs' destiny, indicating not only when the world was supposed to have begun but also when it would end.

At the time of the Spanish conquest, the Aztecs believed they were living in the fifth and final era, which the gods had created 535 years earlier, in AD 986. The square panels around the inner circle (*see diagram*) symbolize destruction of the four previous worlds by jaguars, hurricanes, volcanic fires, and torrential rains. The face inside the circle is that of the sun god, Tonatiuh. The Aztecs were convinced that the world would end on the ritual date "4-movement." But the end came far sooner than expected, with the arrival of Cortés in 1519.

massive rocks. Historically minded Mexicans noted that the sculpture had come to light 269 years to the day after Cortés, the Spanish conquistador, had accepted the surrender of the mighty Aztecs.

The viceroy, Juan Vicente Güemes Pacheco de Padilla, second count of Revillagigedo, took a special interest in the statue and instructed that it be transported to the local university to be weighed, measured, and sketched. In so doing, he reversed a centuries-long Spanish policy of obliterating all vestiges of the vanquished Indian culture, whose artworks were viewed by the Roman Catholic Church as idolatrous, if not satanic.

Within a year, the viceroy's fondness for things archaeological was rewarded with two other major discoveries, again made by laborers engaged in constructing the same public works. First came a carved stone roughly twice as massive as the serpent-entwined statue. Weighing 24 tons, this chunk of gray-black basalt bore a circular relief sculpture some 12 feet in diameter, dominated by a humanlike visage with a protruding knife blade for a tongue. The rest of the stone was embellished with a perplexing assortment of geometric symbols. Dubbed the Stone of the Sun, in part because of its resemblance to a sundial, it was embedded in a pier of the nearby cathedral. (It is often referred to as the Aztec Calendar Stone.)

Next, in 1791, in the northwest corner of the Zócalo, came a prize in the shape of a millstone, which bore a frieze of battling warriors. At the time, it was called the Sacrificial Stone for its supposed purpose, but it is known today as the Stone of Tizoc. It might have been broken up for cobblestones, but an enlightened priest intervened and the relic was given safe berth in the gardens of the cathedral, where it was buried with a single face exposed.

These startling and intriguing finds piqued the interest of scholars, collectors, and ama-

DOOMSDAY
JAGUARS
HURRICANES
SUN GOD

FIRES
RAINS

UNIVERSE

WHAT THE HUB OF THE AZTEC EMPIRE LOOKED LIKE IN 1519

To the Aztecs, their capital was the center not just of the empire but of the world—and at the very heart of it lay the holy precinct where their bloody rituals took place daily. The model below, created for Mexico's National Museum of Anthropology and based on 16th-century Spanish sources as well as on modern finds, shows what the complex probably looked like at the time of the conquest.

Dominating the plaza was the Great Temple. Its twin staircases led to the shrines of Huitzilopochtli, god of the sun and war, and Tlaloc, god of rain, where priests carried out human sacrifices. Flanking the pyramid were several other temples, including a circular one dedicated to Quetzalcoatl, the plumed serpent god; in front of it stood a rack for the skulls of sacrificial victims. Behind Quetzalcoatl's temple lay a court where ritual ball games were played. The large rectangular building to the left housed the *calmecac*, a school for sons of nobles. Around the temples and other buildings ran a wall, setting the religious center off from the rest of the island city.

Published in 1524 from a sketch made for Cortés, this map of Tenochtitlan shows causeways stretching from the religious core to the mainland. A dike, at far right, gave flood protection.

teur archaeologists in Europe. But they would be denied access to them: The failing Spanish empire had all but banned travel in its New World domains and discouraged foreigners from entering the country. Consequently, few outsiders had the chance to examine the finds firsthand. Intellectuals in the United States, busy establishing their new country, paid little if any attention to Mexican antiquities.

The famous German naturalist, Baron Alexander von Humboldt, was one European with enough influence to win entry to Mexico, and his account of his journey there, published in French in 1813, further fanned excitement over Aztec lore. He reported that the Aztecs, hitherto classified as a primitive and nonliterate culture, had actually been highly advanced. When the gates were opened after Mexico gained its independence in 1821, an era of feverish interest in the Aztecs commenced. Tourists, scientists, and adventurers descended on Mexico, then returned to Europe with tales to tell (many of them fanciful), illustrations to publish (a few quite accurate), and, in some cases, trunkfuls of purchased or purloined artifacts.

Among Mexicans, the field of Mesoamerican scholarship was born at the turn of the 19th century, midwifed by the insightful astronomer and archaeologist Antonio de León y Gama. He teased cosmological meanings from the markings on the Stone of the Sun. Some of his readings were false, but he did discover that the Aztecs had sound knowledge of astronomy and a 365-day year. It took a century for others to pin down the identity of the serpent-skirted statue as Coatlicue, goddess of life and death and mother of the fearsome Aztec war god, Huitzilopochtli. Spurred by a newfound pride in their heritage, Mexican anthropologists, historians, and linguists began systematically searching archives, museums, and diverse archaeological sites for clues about the people who had called themselves the "Mexica" or "Tenochca" and ruled with a fierce determination over much of central and southern Mexico.

Ancient cities had been lost before, but perhaps no city had fallen so precipitously and been effaced so thoroughly as the island redoubt of Tenochtitlan. The city was the governmental seat of the Aztecs and the crowning achievement of their 90-year domination of the Valley of Mexico, a high, 3,000-square-mile basin surrounded by mountains. Within a few months of his April 1519 arrival on the Gulf Coast with 600 soldiers and 16 horses, Cortés had imprisoned the Aztec ruler, Motecuhzoma Xocoyotzin. (The Spaniards inaccurately rendered his first name, meaning Angry Lord, as Montezuma, and over the years he has also often been wrongly referred to as Moctezuma.) Less than two years after his arrival, the conquistador Cortés and his band of soldiers, with the much-needed help of Indian warriors from cities eager to throw off the Aztecs' yoke of forced tribute, had toppled Motecuhzoma, razed his capital and other cities in his empire, and claimed the rest of his far-flung territories. Cortés took control of the lives and fortunes of perhaps as many as 11 million Aztecs and their subject peoples.

Only a few generations later, the brilliant accomplishments of the Aztecs had all but vanished from Mexico's memory, and no one was sure just where the key structures of Tenochtitlan had stood. For example, by the 18th century, popular opinion held that the ruins of *el Templo Mayor,* or the Great Temple, the Aztec nation's principal shrine, lay directly under the cathedral. This was a convenient myth for those wishing to promote an image of Christianity triumphant. Gone also from common awareness was knowledge of the intricate religion of the Aztecs and an understanding of their highly evolved symbology, which had enabled them to express their beliefs in a fashion as potent and accessible to their minds as the crucifix was to Cortés and his contemporaries.

So powerful were the Aztecs' icons, in fact, that the best intentions of later scholars could not always succeed in removing the clergy's fear of them—and of the impact they might have on Mexicans of Indian blood. The Coatlicue statue dug up in front of the National Palace saw the light of day only briefly at its supposed haven in the university. As Humboldt explained: "The professors, at that time Dominican priests, did not want to exhibit this idol to the Mexican youth, so they buried it again in one of the halls of the building." Subsequently, the statue was dug up for Humboldt's visit, then rapidly reburied. It remained interred until 1823, when it was consigned to an infrequently used corridor in the National Museum. In fact, the Coatlicue story serves as a telling metaphor for the entire Aztec culture, which was repeatedly suppressed and submerged in the centuries after the Spanish conquest, only to be disinterred and brought to light again. Tenochtitlan and its inhabitants refused to slip quietly into oblivion.

For many years, any desire to gain a more tangible picture of the Aztec capital as it existed on the eve of the conquest ran up against an insurmountable obstacle—the terrible devastation wrought by Cortés's army. Today, the effort is hampered by the fact that the remains of Tenochtitlan and its many satellite communities lie buried beneath the smoggy, sprawling metropolis of more than eight million people that is Mexico City proper. Therefore, comprehensive excavations like those undertaken at other Mesoamerican sites, such as the Maya city of Chichen Itza and the pre-Aztec Teotihuacan, just 25 miles northeast of the Mexican capital, have been impossible. Many of the major digs since the early part of this century—when archaeology came into its own—have been initiated by chance. Just as in 1790, artifacts have accidentally turned up in the course of construction projects—for example, during the building of sewer lines in 1900 and the subway system in the 1960s and 1970s. After hurriedly deploying at such sites, archaeologists have been forced to excavate at lightning pace, hastening to rescue what they could before work resumed on the projects. Fortunately, although the remains of Tenochtitlan itself only rarely become accessible for examination, archaeologists have been able to gain a remarkably vivid view of the city at the height of its grandeur by drawing on an array of narratives composed in and around the time of Cortés's victory. Gradually, haphazard finds have given way to more organized searches, guided by this written material.

Rarely have archaeologists been given a script as complete as the body of work that has helped direct their excavations of the Aztec capital. Spanish priests, conquistadors, and the Aztecs themselves (via codices, or annals, produced at the priests' urgings) left behind a bright light that can be shone into the gloom of their wrecked and buried civilization. Among the documents are letters by Cortés himself to Charles V, the Holy Roman Emperor, accounts by several of the soldiers who were involved in the conquest, and histories composed by Spanish friars. Cortés's letters to his king were written in

Gods and mortals march across the accordion-folded pages of the Codex Fejérváry Mayer. Codices were painted on leather panels, like this one, or on bark paper. The Indians—who lacked a written language—used the pictures to help them remember details when reciting their intricate myths.

some measure as an insurance policy: Having abandoned his allegiance to his superior, the governor of Cuba, Cortés hoped to appeal directly to the Spanish crown to avoid possible punishment. His ploy was to offer Charles a share of any booty he might seize over and above the customary "royal fifth" provided by other explorers. Along with narratives by his cohorts, Cortés's letters help provide both a panoramic depiction of the epochal events of 1519 and a valuable look at daily life in the Aztec capital.

Little Aztec literature from preconquest days has survived. In the 16th century, as the Spanish government struggled to consolidate its power over the Indians, Juan de Zumárraga, founding archbishop of Mexico, ordered huge quantities of native art and literature rounded up and burned. But in the decades that followed, a handful of enlightened Spaniards worked quietly to preserve the scant remaining evidence of native culture. Thanks to the Aztecs' rich oral tradition, they were able to rescue much of what would have been lost in another generation or two.

One of the great ironies of the conquest is that from the ranks of the Roman Catholic Church, the very institution that led the charge to destroy the Aztec legacy, came the principal agents of preservation. Occasionally drawing funds from the official coffers of the Church but more often making do with limited resources, several dedicated missionaries, including especially the Franciscan friar Bernardino de Sahagún, attempted to recapture the intellectual heritage of the Aztecs before the last generation of Indians to have lived under Motecuhzoma passed away.

The brilliant and tenacious Sahagún oversaw the production of one of the most famous and profusely illustrated Aztec codices, often referred to as the Florentine Codex, after the Italian city in which it resides today. Sahagún had come to Mexico in his youth and had rapidly become fluent in Nahuatl, the Aztec tongue. In his dealings with the Indians, he became convinced that "idolatrous superstitions, auguries, abuses, and idolatrous ceremonies are not yet completely lost." Consequently, it was necessary for missionaries to learn about the Aztec religion in order to better recognize and stamp

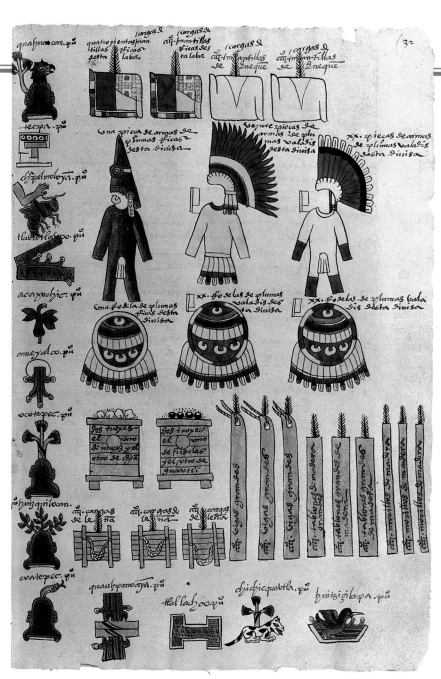

out practices and habits of mind that were holdovers from pagan times. His motives aside, Sahagún operated in a highly objective fashion, gathering information with techniques that closely resemble those used by modern anthropologists. He carried out extensive interviews with Aztec informants, while native scribes recorded the data. The result, which goes by its official name, the *General History of the Things of New Spain,* is a rich source of material about Aztec culture.

Another text produced in similar fashion, the *History of the Indies of New Spain,* written by the Dominican friar Diego Durán, offers another detailed, and sympathetic, portrait of the Aztecs. Completed in 1581, shipped to Spain, and forgotten, Durán's *History* was rediscovered and copied in the mid-1800s, although it had been altered and defaced over the years, probably by censorious monks. For the sake of being true to the Indian point of view, Durán wrote, he had been impelled to describe, "together with good and heroic actions, Cortés's frightful and cruel atrocities, his completely inhuman acts."

With Aztec assistants and informants, the friars compiled dictionaries and glossaries of Nahuatl, which was then a spoken, not a written, language, as well as versions of the Aztecs' codices, brightly painted, accordion-folded books. The codices, now treasures of museums and libraries in Europe, North America, and Mexico, illustrate elaborate ceremonial scenes and carry notations in a pictographic system made up of glyphs, symbols that stand not so much for words as for sets of related concepts. In practice, the codices served mainly as memory prompts. Like the originals, many of the 16th- and 17th-

A list of tribute to be paid the Aztecs includes the 13 contributing communities, identified by glyphs in the left and bottom margins of a page from a codex, as well as the items. The two plain rectangles in the two top rows represent the number of large mantles given, with each feather standing for 400 mantles—or 800 mantles in all. The Aztecs used dots for numbers between 1 and 19, and pennants for 20 and its multiples (right). They rendered a large number, such as 8,000, as a bulging bag of cacao beans.

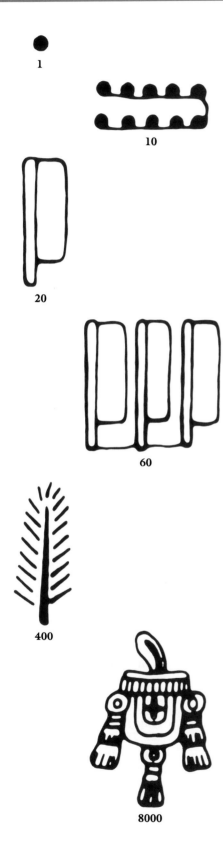

1

10

20

60

400

8000

century replicas were inscribed on sheets of deerskin or bark paper. The vivid texts and pictures of the codices offer insights not only into the distant Aztec past but also into the period directly preceding the arrival of Cortés. The panels portray elaborately costumed priests and noblemen, Aztec victories over neighboring tribes, tales of the gods, and scenes of the epochal arrival of the Spaniards and their eventual destruction of Aztec culture.

By 1519, designated as the year 1 Reed on the Aztec calendar, buildings erected over many generations covered a once-uninhabited island in the southwest corner of broad, marshy Lake Tetzcoco with a dazzling array of temples, palaces, homes for the upper classes, and public forums. There were also thousands of lesser abodes for artisans, merchants, and other members of the highly stratified Aztec society. Tenochtitlan, with perhaps as many as 200,000 inhabitants, was the center of a wide-ranging territory over which the Aztecs exerted brutal control.

The Aztecs, almost constantly at war with someone, exacted animal skins, precious stones, copper and gold, cotton, foodstuffs, and other raw materials and products as tribute from those they vanquished. In addition to captives they took on the battlefield, they also demanded a yearly ransom of victims for sacrifice to the war god, Huitzilopochtli, and the rain god, Tlaloc.

In rising to suzerainty over the peoples of the Valley of Mexico, the Aztecs had overcome more than a century of hardship. According to their own legends, their ancestors had heeded a divine command to leave their paradisiacal island homeland, Aztlan, translated as "the place of the herons," which scholars think may have been located in northwestern Mexico. Wandering for more than a century in the harsh desert, scrabbling a meager living from the arid land, the Aztecs, or "people of Aztlan," had finally arrived in the densely settled valley sometime toward the end of the 12th century. Finding themselves reviled squatters and outcasts there, forced sometimes to suffer periods of servitude, the bellicose Aztecs had eventually triumphed over scores of enemy city-states. With an implacable will, a well-tooled war-making machinery, a high degree of social cohesion, and a flair for cultural appropriation, they had gone on to forge a civilization rivaling those that had flourished millennia earlier in Egypt and Mesopotamia, and in a far shorter time.

The Aztecs' tragic flaw, perhaps, was their fatalism. Indeed, their destiny was set forever when Cortés left Cuba, where he had lived for eight years, in February 1519. The island's governor, Diego Velásquez, had appointed Cortés to lead an expedition in search of new sources of slaves and treasure for Spain. But as Cortés mustered his troops and supplies, Velásquez began to worry that the ambitious younger man would overreach his authority. Hearing of his mentor's doubts, Cortés confirmed them by casting off earlier than scheduled. First he probed the Yucatan coast, then sailed westward to put in, finally, at a location he dubbed Villa Rica de la Vera Cruz (present-day Veracruz), "rich town of the true Cross."

It was in Veracruz that Cortés first learned of the fabulous treasures that, from then on, beckoned to him from the interior. As was to happen so often in the coming months, the Aztecs' own actions, stemming from their extremely limited view of the world beyond their borders, abetted and hastened their downfall. In this case, a misguided attempt at diplomacy would bring calamity. Motecuhzoma had sent several groups of envoys with offerings that included regal vestments of the style the Aztec gods were thought to wear. But it was their gold that caught the conqueror's eye. Rather than appeasing him, the emissaries merely whetted his appetite for wealth and confirmed him in his determination to march on.

Setting out with his army from Veracruz, Cortés made the arduous trek from the tropical coastal lowlands up into the mountains with about 400 men, two-thirds of his army. There the Spaniards encountered Tlaxcalan warriors. The Tlaxcalans had maintained independence from the Aztecs where others had failed. Their brightly attired warriors mobbed the Spanish interlopers in several bitter engagements, but, thanks to his cannon and horses, Cortés prevailed. With breathtaking expediency, the Tlaxcalans presented Cortés token gifts of cloth, semiprecious stones, and gold, and offered to lead him onward to the Aztec stronghold.

Through two interpreters, an Indian woman named Marina, who spoke both Nahuatl and one of the Maya languages, and a shipwrecked Spaniard picked up in Yucatan, Jerónimo de Aguilar, who was also fluent in Maya, Cortés gathered intelligence on his future adversary, Motecuhzoma. Marina had come to Cortés as part of the spoils of an earlier fray with the Indians along the Tabasco coast, and her intelligence and skills in Nahuatl proved invaluable—so much so that it is doubtful Cortés would have succeeded without her. It was lucky, too, that she and Aguilar understood similar Maya dialects, which facilitated the three-step process of communication, Nahuatl to Maya to Spanish, then back again.

While Cortés was camped in Tlaxcala, he was visited by more tribute-bearing envoys sent by Motecuhzoma to persuade the Spaniards to turn back and to dissuade them from making an alliance with the Aztecs' old enemies. Almost from the moment the Spaniards had debarked in Veracruz, Aztec emissaries had been watching them closely, relaying information on their movements to Tenochtitlan. As the Spaniards advanced, Motecuhzoma's spies took their measure as adversaries and provided the ruler with small paintings of the invaders, showing their metal-covered heads and odd attire, their tame "deer" that carried them "wherever they wish to go, holding them as high as the roof of a house," and their war dogs, "savage, like demons, always bounding about." Cortés had taken every opportunity to impress his authority upon the Indians. Witnessing a demonstration of Spanish cannon fire, some messengers had even fainted.

Cortés, unrelenting, and guided by the Aztec ambassadors, moved on toward the coveted wealth of Tenochtitlan, taking some Tlaxcalan warriors with him. In nearby Cholula, a mercantile city in alliance with Motecuhzoma and the religious seat of the plumed serpent god, Quetzalcoatl, Cortés's invaluable companion, Doña Marina, warned him that the Cholulans were conspiring against him. As a result, the Spaniards and their Tlaxcalan henchmen massacred thousands of men, women, and children, casting down idols from the temples in their ruthless attack.

From the accounts recorded by the Aztecs themselves in the codices prepared under the friars, it is clear that Motecuhzoma had long dreaded the arrival of powerful men from the east. Legend foretold the return of Quetzalcoatl, who generations before had departed Mexico on a raft woven of serpents, promising to return one day to reclaim his throne. The predicted year of his second coming was to be 1 Reed on the Aztec calendar—as capricious fate would have it, the very year of Cortés's arrival.

As soon as he got word of Spanish ships—the supposed giant raft of Quetzalcoatl—plying the coast, the bewildered, anxious, and superstitious Motecuhzoma feared he was doomed. Obsessed with the old prophecy, he prepared to surrender his empire. A series of menacing portents had convinced him that he was destined to preside over the destruction of Aztec civilization. So disturbed was Motecuhzoma, reported Friar Durán on the evidence of Aztec witnesses, that "he was half desirous that the events which had been predicted take place immediately."

The omens that had unnerved Motecuhzoma gripped his people with anxiety. According to one Aztec codex, nightly for a year "there arose a sign like a tongue of fire, like a flame. Pointed and wide-based, it pierced the heavens to their midpoint, their very heart. All night, off to the east, it looked as if day had dawned. Then the sun arose and destroyed it." A temple inexplicably burst into flames, and the fire could not be extinguished. On a calm day, lightning struck the roof of another temple. A large column of light was seen in the east. A comet appeared one afternoon, hurtling from west to east and "scattering sparks like glowing coals." Lake Tetzcoco was suddenly roiled to flood heights, for no apparent reason. And at night, people claimed to have heard a woman weeping. "She would pace about wailing, 'My dear children, we have to go! Where can I take you?' " (It is unlikely that these phenomena had any sound astronomical or geological basis. Some scholars suggest that the awesome events were exaggerated by the Aztecs who told of them in later years.)

When all of the bribes, incantations, and pleas of his emissaries failed to halt the Spaniards' march on his city, Motecuhzoma panicked. As a last resort, the "Angry Lord" attempted to flee, according to Durán, but Aztec priests waylaid him and pressured him

PICTURING THE FINAL DAYS OF A ONCE-MIGHTY EMPIRE

For nearly 50 years, the Franciscan friar and missionary Bernardino de Sahagún studied the Aztecs with a sympathetic but objective eye. His masterwork, the Florentine Codex, records the accounts of the Aztecs themselves and details Indian customs and the conquest in both Nahuatl, the Aztec tongue, and Spanish. The Inquisition confiscated the codex in 1577 as pro-Indian, and it was suppressed for some 200 years. Portions of the document are reproduced at right and overleaf.

The story begins with the arrival of Hernán Cortés, whom the Aztecs believed to be the feathered serpent god, Quetzalcoatl. In their mythology, this deity—who had been forced to leave his people—would one day return and bring with him a new way of life.

As the Spaniards disembark, Indians arrive. "They went as if to sell goods," says the codex, "in order to go spy upon them." Asked by the strangers where they lived, the Aztecs replied, "It is from there in Mexico that we have come."

to return. Certain even before the fact that his reign had come to an end, Motecuhzoma gave a farewell speech. "With abundant tears he cried out to the masses that he was terrified over the arrival of the strangers," reported Durán. After this public scene, the king returned to the palace and "bade farewell to his wives and children with sorrow and tears, charging all his attendants to care for his family, since he considered himself a man about to die."

It was November 1519. Cortés sat astride his horse looking out on the city he intended to possess. Nearby was Bernal Díaz del Castillo, who, many years later, in his 70s, recounted his impressions of that day in the *True History of the Conquest of Mexico*. Now half-blind and partly deaf, Díaz remembered the sights and sounds of his youth with amazing clarity.

The view from just outside Tenochtitlan was impressive. "When we beheld so many cities and towns on the water, and other large settlements built on firm ground, and that broad causeway running so straight and perfectly level to the city of Tenochtitlan," Díaz wrote, "we were astonished because of the great stone towers and temples and buildings that rose up out of the water. Some of our soldiers said that all these things seemed to be a dream; and it is no wonder that I write here in this manner, for never was there seen, nor

Aztec emissaries bear gifts to Cortés, whose coming was presaged by various omens. Motecuhzoma, their ruler, offered the Spaniard an annual tribute of whatever he desired if he would not enter Tenochtitlan, the capital.

Having entered the capital and put Motecuhzoma under arrest, the Spaniards discover the Aztec treasure behind a plastered wall in a palace storeroom. The greedy Spaniards, reports the codex, "took all, all that they saw which they saw to be good."

Preparing for a festival, worshipers in front of a temple make offerings to the war god, Huitzilopochtli.

heard, nor even dreamt, anything like that which we then observed." The strangers descended on the capital. "They came," wrote an Aztec witness, "in battle array, as conquerors, and the dust rose in whirlwinds on the roads, their spears glinted in the sun, and their pennons fluttered like bats. Some of them were dressed in glistening iron from head to foot; they terrified everyone who saw them." Throngs of Aztecs, nervous but curious, poured out of their homes to observe the Spaniards, some of them lining the causeway—one of three connecting Tenochtitlan to the mainland—and others darting across the surface of Lake Tetzcoco in canoes.

Not far from the city the Spanish forces stopped, met by a procession of the royal household. It was Motecuhzoma, wrote Díaz, borne "beneath a marvelously rich canopy of green-colored feathers with intricate patterns in gold and silver and with pearls and green chalcolite stones hanging from a sort of embroidery that was wonderful to behold. And the great Motecuhzoma was richly attired according to his practice, and he was shod with sandals, the soles of gold and the upper part adorned with precious stones."

Motecuhzoma got down from his litter, reported Díaz, and none of the lords accompanying him, except those supporting him ceremonially as he walked, "dared even to think of looking directly at his face" but kept their eyes averted. Heeding his cue, Cortés

The Spaniards massacre participants in the feast of Huitzilopochtli. "Blood ran like water," laments the codex.

The triumphant conquistadors cast out the bodies of Motecuhzoma and a nobleman.

Cortés's army flees Tenochtitlan after Motecuhzoma's death set off a revolt; more than 800 Spaniards died.

dismounted and approached the Aztec ruler, offering his hand, which Motecuhzoma declined. Cortés persisted, presenting Motecuhzoma with a necklace of pearly margarite beads; but when he made as if to embrace the king, said Díaz, "those great lords who accompanied Motecuhzoma held back the arm of Cortés so that he should not embrace him, for they considered it an indignity." When these formalities were over, Cortés and his men were escorted into Tenochtitlan and lodged in a commodious palace that had belonged to Motecuhzoma's father. The city that Nahuatl poets had described as a "great domed tree, precious as jade," which radiated "flashes of light like quetzal plumes," had been violated by sinister strangers.

After just one week, Cortés executed a bizarre, bloodless coup. Citing a clash at Veracruz in which several of his men had been killed, Cortés told Motecuhzoma that under pain of death he would have to come with him to the Spaniards' lodging. As the Aztec ruler was led through the streets, he told his agitated people that he was going of his own free will. From then on, Motecuhzoma was little more than a pitiable reciter of proclamations, a ruler in name only while Cortés pulled his strings.

Oddly, the men who were to destroy Tenochtitlan appreciated its beauty and elegant engineering, for it was more magnificent than many European cities of the time, including, said some well-

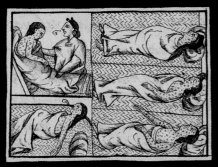

An Aztec physician attends a smallpox patient. The disease, introduced by the Spaniards, killed one-third of the Indians, including Cuitlahuac, Motecuhzoma's brother and successor.

Eleven months after they fled, the Spaniards return to Tenochtitlan. Cortés surrounded the city, destroying its aqueducts and thus vanquishing its people.

The Spaniards burn the temple at Tlatelolco, last center of resistance. "There was plundering, then there was capturing of the poor common folk," says the codex.

traveled conquista-
dors, Rome and Constanti-
nople. The largely deforested
and overgrazed European landscape
hosted cities on a smaller scale, which still
bore the stamp of a constrained medieval sensibility. In western
Europe, only London, Rome, and Venice boasted populations of
anywhere near 100,000. Seville, with an estimated population of
60,000, was closest in size of any Spanish city to Tenochtitlan, whose
population was estimated at 200,000. It must have galled the Spaniards that pagans—people who were not even mentioned in the
Bible—had constructed a city that excelled any of theirs.

León y Gama, who has been called the father of Mexican

Composed of prized green quetzal and blue cotinga feathers and gold disks (detail, right), this four-foot-high headdress is popularly regarded as Motecuhzoma's. It was sent to Europe soon after the conquest, but whether it actually belonged to the Aztec ruler is not known.

archaeology, would argue that the Aztecs had to have been remarkable artisans to have hewn their elaborate architectural ornamentations and "feigned images," or idols, using only primitive stone tools. Furthermore, while entirely ignorant of the principle of the arch, they had built on a monumental scale. And they had laid out Tenochtitlan with consummate skill. They were, in short, possessed of vast knowledge "in arts and sciences in the time of their heathendom," he wrote. Cortés marveled over Tenochtitlan's large and beautiful temples and houses, its grid of streets and interlacing canals, its clean layout with four quadrants meeting at a central square.

Motecuhzoma's palace was decorated with murals, bas-reliefs, ornate woven cloths, golden screens to keep the king from being seen while he ate, and with cedar beams carved, according to Cortés, with "ornamental borders of flowers, birds, and fish." The Spaniards toured the ruler's large and impressive private zoo, which housed animals of nearly every species in Middle America, including jaguars and tapirs, rattlesnakes in feather-lined jars, an aviary, and gardens.

Although an uneasy balance of affairs continued during the six months after the Spaniards' arrival, existence went on in the capital, and Cortés and his men had the opportunity to observe, close up, the Aztec way of life. In his second letter to Charles V, Cortés described the city's setting. In the basin, he wrote, there "are two lakes that almost fill it. One of these two lakes is of fresh water and the other, which is larger, is salty. From one lake to another and among the cities and other settlements that are about said lakes, communication is by canoe, with no need of going overland."

Cortés went on to describe the city's situation. "From any direction one may wish to enter, the city is two leagues from the shore. It has four entrances, each an artificial causeway two short lance lengths in width. Its main streets are very wide and straight. Some of these and all the others are half solid roadway and half canal for canoe traffic. All the streets are open at intervals where canals join. But in all these gaps, some of which are very broad, there are bridges made of great, wide, shaped, close-set beams. On many of these, 10 horses could walk abreast."

Dominating the city, the 150-foot pyramid of the Great Temple loomed over this network of busy waterways and streets. While reviling the idolatry of the Aztecs, Cortés could not help being awed by the achievements of their architects. He marveled at the beauty of the temples and the buildings that housed the idols, and he commented on the quality of the priests' quarters. He was struck by the priests' appearance; they wore black, he reported, "and they neither cut nor comb their hair from the time they enter the priesthood until they leave it." He all but gave up trying to describe adequately the religious center at the city's core: "It is so large that in its precincts, which are surrounded by a wall, there could well lie a settlement of five hundred. Inside this area, about its edges, are fine buildings with large halls and corridors. There are at least 40 pyramids, very tall and well made; the largest has 50 steps leading up to the main body of the pyramid. The principal pyramid is taller than the Seville Cathedral's tower. The stone masonry and the woodwork are equally good; they could nowhere be bettered. All the stonework inside the temples where they keep the idols is sculptured, and the woodwork is all carved in relief and painted with pictures of monsters and other figures and designs."

Cortés could not have failed to notice another feature of the temple complex. The Aztecs showed a fascination with the heads of their victims, preserving them on skull racks in front of the temples. Díaz guessed that some tens of thousands of skulls crowded the racks. Two conquistadors who counted them put the number at more than 136,000. Some of them still oozing blood, others already bleached by the sun, they were in every stage of decomposition.

The Aztecs' fondness for sacrifice displayed itself in another way. The steps of the twin stairways leading to the lofty platform atop the Great Pyramid where victims' hearts were cut out were black with dried blood. At the summit, Huitzilopochtli's shrine had a painted facade embedded with bands of skulls. The adjacent Tlaloc's shrine was striped with bands of blue representing water. In open view at the head of the staircases, the priests, with blood-matted hair and bodies scarred by ritu-

IN THE KINGDOM OF THE ANIMALS

Living close to nature as they did, the Aztecs saw in many animals—including insects—qualities to emulate, and even attributed supernatural powers to several. They used various creatures in their art to express or symbolize attitudes and beliefs. Motecuhzoma himself kept wild animals; his

zoo was so large 300 workers looked after it. According to Cortés, the collection contained "a bird of prey of every sort," and caged jaguars, wolves, foxes, and cats "that were given as many turkeys to eat as they needed" as well as the remains of human sacrifices.

Aztec artists regularly produced animal figures to adorn temples and palaces. The sculptor who carved the basalt eagle above for the Great Temple probably did so for the warriors known as the Eagle Knights, who chose this fierce bird, recognized as a symbol of the sun, as their emblem and guiding spirit. The jaguar *(below, left)* was the totem of the Jaguar Knights. The largest predator of the Middle American jungle, the cat embodied power and courage and came to be associated directly with the Aztec ruler, whose patron it was.

The snake had multiple aspects. Its undulating movements suggested both water and fertility. And because it shed its skin, it also represented renewal and change. The granite coiled rattlesnake above is typical for its precise detail: The bottom is as carefully rendered as the top.

On the lighter side, the Aztecs saw the monkey as the personification of mischief, gluttony, and lechery. This one, carved of basalt, holds a flower in one hand, while its chest bears the *xopilcozcatl,* symbol for a claw-shaped jewel.

ally inflicted wounds, plied their gruesome trade. Stepping into the blood-encrusted shrine to Huitzilopochtli, Díaz was shocked and revulsed. "In that small space," he wrote, "there were many diabolical things to be seen, bugles and trumpets and knives, and many hearts of Indians that they had burned in fumigating their idols, and everything was so clotted with blood, and there was so much of it, that I curse the whole of it, and as it stank like a slaughterhouse we hastened to clear out of such a bad stench and worse sight."

Both Cortés and Díaz reported that the Spaniards witnessed human sacrifices committed by priests armed with mosaic sacrificial knives. "Whenever they wish to ask something of the idols," wrote Cortés, "they take many girls and boys and even adults, and in the presence of the idols they open their chests while they are still alive and take out their hearts and entrails and burn them before the idols, offering the smoke as sacrifice. Some of us have seen this, and they say it is the most terrible and frightful thing they have ever witnessed. Not one year passes in which they do not kill and sacrifice some 50 persons in each temple."

The Spanish chronicler Durán, working from information provided by Aztecs, provided a more detailed account of the way in which the killing was performed. Awaiting the victims at the top of the pyramid stood six robed priests, their faces smeared black with soot and their heads encircled in leather bands. One carried a wooden yoke carved in the form of a snake. "They seized the victims one by one, one by one foot, another by the other, one priest by one hand, and another by the other hand," he wrote. "The victim was thrown on his back, upon the pointed stone, where the wretch was grabbed by the fifth priest, who placed the yoke upon his throat. The high priest then opened the chest and with amazing swiftness tore out the heart, ripping it out with his own hands. Thus steaming, the heart was lifted toward the sun, and the fumes were offered up to the sun. The priest then turned toward the idol and cast the heart in its face. After the heart had been extracted, the body was allowed to roll down the steps of the pyramid. Between the sacrificial stone and the beginning of the steps there was a distance of no more than two feet."

29

Despite their bloody religious customs, the Aztecs struck Cortés in the main as a people who comported themselves with civility. Their "activities and behavior," he conceded, "are on almost as high a level as in Spain. Considering that these people are barbarous, lacking knowledge of God and communication with other civilized nations, it is remarkable to see all that they have."

Cortés, ambitious to the point of recklessness, had gambled all to take his tiny band of men and horses into the capital of an empire renowned for its military prowess. But he was driven by dreams of wealth, power, fame, and spreading the gospel.

Sculpted rocks and mutilated figures of Aztec deities and rulers are all that remain of Motecuhzoma's temple and gardens at Chapultepec, or "grasshopper hill," in the suburbs of Tenochtitlan. The 18.6-inch-long, carneolite grasshopper (top) was unearthed at the site in 1785 during the building of a castle.

The Indians valued gold but did not covet it, and one Aztec was transfixed by the behavior of a group of Spaniards in the presence of gold. They picked it up, he reported, "and fingered it like monkeys: They seemed transported by joy, as if their hearts were illuminated and made new. They hungered like pigs for that gold." Cortés himself told an emissary of Motecuhzoma that his people were stricken by a "disease of the heart which can only be cured by gold."

As for power, Cortés sought it with guile and cunning, knowing himself overwhelmingly outnumbered. He took care not to provoke the Aztecs, using Motecuhzoma as his mouthpiece and endeavoring at every turn to placate rather than rile the king's closest advisers and lieutenants, who had begun to agitate against the Span-

30

iards. But in April, after having spent six months in the capital, Cortés was forced to deal with a crisis at his rear. A disciplinary force under the command of Pánfilo de Narváez had been sent from Cuba by Velásquez. Cortés hurried back to his outpost at Veracruz, where he bribed Narváez's soldiers with jewels and gold, winning their allegiance to the point where he could overcome their leader.

In Cortés's absence, the temporary commander in Tenochtitlan, Pedro de Alvarado, brashly launched an attack on unarmed Aztecs, apparently caving in to fears of a rumored Aztec uprising. On the pretext of observing an Aztec ceremony dedicated to Huitzilopochtli, Alvarado sent his men into the temple precinct. The occasion drew, Durán guessed, 8,000 to 10,000 Aztec warriors to the walled precinct, all splendidly bedecked and dancing to the beat of numerous drums. Suddenly, Spanish soldiers massed in the narrow doorways and swiftly set upon the celebrants. According to Aztec accounts, "They first struck a drummer; they severed both his hands and cut off his head, which fell to the ground some distance away." Next, they butchered the crowds. "Everywhere were intestines, severed heads, hands, and feet. The dreadful screams and lamentations in that patio! And no one there to aid them!"

By the time Cortés had rushed back from the coast with reinforcements, the city was in revolt. Cortés attempted to soothe the citizenry by bringing Motecuhzoma before them, but when the Aztec leader attempted to reason with the assembled masses, promising that the Spaniards would leave Mexico, they jeered and threw stones. Most Spanish accounts of this incident attributed Motecuhzoma's subsequent death to the stones, but Durán's informants reported that the Aztec ruler was found with five dagger wounds, presumably inflicted by the desperate Spaniards.

The Aztec forces, enraged by the death of Motecuhzoma and vastly superior in numbers to the Spaniards, sent the conquistadors into pell-mell retreat. During the terrible *Noche Triste,* or Night of Sorrow, June 30, 1520, Cortés lost 800 men and was driven with his survivors out of the capital and all the way back to Tlaxcala. The Aztecs attacked on foot and by canoe, mercilessly pursuing the despised Spaniards. But, skilled as they were at the art of war, the Aztecs committed a fatal error in this as in all their clashes with the Spaniards. Aztec warriors held as their ultimate goal not slaying the enemy but capturing him alive. This sprang from the need to provide always more fodder for the ravening Huitzilopochtli. Time and again in the final battles over Tenochtitlan, Spanish soldiers benefited from this strategic predisposition. Instead of fighting to kill, the Aztecs fought to imprison the enemy. Had the Aztec warriors gone for the battlefield kill—and had they cultivated better relations with their neighbors and been able to turn to them for help—Cortés's army might ultimately have been destroyed.

The Aztecs had won, but only for a time. Cortés spent 10 months regrouping, then returned with a formidable alliance of Spanish and Tlaxcalan soldiers. He had hardened his heart. "When I saw how rebellious the people of this city were, and how they seemed more determined to perish than any race of man known before," he wrote, "I did not know by what means we might relieve ourselves of all these dangers and hardships, and yet avoid destroying them and their city, which was indeed the most beautiful thing in the world."

Defeat for the Aztecs thus came with a vengeance. All their menacing finery of jaguar skins and eagle feathers and their bellicose brandishing of spears and clublike, obsidian-edged wooden swords was little more than a colorful and futile show. Like scythes, the Spaniards cut down perhaps two-thirds of the people of Tenochtitlan, and the rest surrendered. After a siege of 75 days, Cortés stood triumphant, securing for Spain—and for himself—the vast territory owing fealty to Tenochtitlan.

Thus a robust, highly cultured, wealthy, and advancing civilization which, by all appearances, had not yet reached its zenith, ended swiftly and violently. In the heat of the final battle, Cortés ordered his soldiers to raze the enemy city as they went. The conquistadors smashed statues, pulled down walls and lintels, and sacked and demolished temples amid billowing clouds of smoke from burning houses. Spanish violence and despotism would continue to devastate the defeated population for a very long time. Famine and disease, especially smallpox, which the Spaniards carried and against which the Indians had no resistance, compounded the Aztecs' plight.

"There is nothing but grief and suffering in Mexico and Tlatelolco, where once we saw beauty and valor," wrote a Nahuatl poet. "Have you grown weary of your servants? Are you angry with your servants, O Giver of Life?" he implored the god Huitzilopochtli. Another poet, anonymous now, stripped of identity by defeat, lamented the tremendous loss: "Broken spears lie in the roads; we have torn our hair in grief. The houses are roofless now, and their walls are red with blood. We have pounded our heads in despair against the adobe walls, for our inheritance, our city, is lost and dead. The shields of our warriors were its defense, but they could not save it."

The toppled stones of Tenochtitlan and its sister city, Tlate-lolco, became the building blocks of Mexico City. Over a period of time the Spaniards broke up hand-hewn monoliths or tipped them into place whole to form foundations, abutments, or other supports. They dumped rubble and fill into Tenochtitlan's extensive system of canals, which had made the city a veritable Venice of the Americas. They gradually drained Lake Tetzcoco and ruined most of the *chinampas,* fertile "floating garden" plots upon which farmers had raised crops of corn, squash, amaranth—a highly productive, protein-rich grain that was an important staple—beans, and chilies, and the flowers that had been ubiquitous in Aztec life and ceremony. They even banned the use of amaranth in the diet.

Meanwhile, church authorities waged a demolition campaign against all manifestations of paganism, ordering Indian books, religious items, and statuary destroyed. Those items too large to be removed were mutilated. Over the remains of Motecuhzoma's once-glorious abode rose the edifice of the Spanish-colonial mint and the National Palace, and atop the leveled precincts of the Great Temple, where Aztec priests had sacrificed thousands of human victims, the burgeoning colonial city spread.

Inscribed on the Stone of the Sun are four images signifying a jaguar, the wind, fiery rain, and water. The images stand for the dates of the end of each of the four previous Aztec ages, called suns. At the center of the stone sits a fifth calendric symbol, the face of Tonatiuh, the sun god. Archaeologists now know that the Aztecs believed they were living in the time of the fifth and last sun. The four earlier ones had been destroyed in cataclysms at the time of the four dates depicted on the stone. So too, said the Aztec priests, the fifth age was sure to end violently. As the Spaniards toured the wrecked streets of Tenochtitlan, sickened by the stench of rotting corpses, the Stone of the Sun was already sinking into the soft soil of the island redoubt. The horror foreseen by the priests had come to pass.

THE TREK TO DESTINY

The Aztecs had reason to be proud of themselves. In less than 200 years, they had risen from their humble origins as a nomadic tribe to become supreme masters of the Valley of Mexico and regions beyond. They attributed their success to the blessing of their god and patron, Huitzilopochtli, and fashioned a myth that glorified their years of wandering in the desert. This is a story they loved to tell, and they did so often, with unabashed gusto and relish. Children learned it at school. Bards recited it in verse. And artists set it down in bark-paper books known as codices, where the tale unfolds in a series of pictures and glyphs.

As depicted in the surviving codices, the Aztec rise to glory began in the arid cactus lands northwest of the Valley of Mexico, at a place called Chicomoztoc, or Seven Caverns, in a cave in the hill of Colhuatepec *(opposite)*. The setting was mythic: Other tribes, as well as the Toltecs before them, claimed the same place of origin. Why the Aztecs left the region is anybody's guess. In all likelihood they were driven out by local overlords, although they preferred to believe that Huitzilopochtli foreordained their departure. As the Aztecs slowly migrated southward toward the valley, legend hardened into fact; by the time they reached the place that was to be their capital—signaled by an eagle atop a cactus *(above)*—each episode could be pinned down by date and appropriate pictorial detail.

Although there once were thousands of Aztec codices, no originals from the days before the Spanish conquest apparently survive. The Spaniards, in their eagerness to snuff out pagan beliefs, destroyed most of them. Even so, among some of the Indians the codex tradition continued for a while longer. Occasionally encouraged by a few sympathetic Spaniards, they left a record that re-created aspects of the Aztec myth, including the fascinating examples on the following pages.

Emerging from the womblike interior of Colhuatepec, supposed birthplace of the Aztecs and
related tribes, two leaders of the Chichimec
tribe parley with two feather-clad Toltecs. The
commalike marks flowing between the men in
the foreground stand for speech. Represented by
heads and identified by tribal glyphs, other Indians are seen in the cave. The coyote-robed
figure at upper right lights a ceremonial fire,
a sign that great things are about to happen.

he story of their beginnings, the Aztecs liked
n the purity and holiness of their ancestors. In
on of the chronicle, recorded on a 15-foot-
of fig-bark paper called the Codex Boturini,
t Aztec forebears are shown living a modest,
stence on an island in the middle of a lake—
ly Aztlan, the traditional Aztec tribal home-
n which their name derives. A temple pyramid
by six stylized dwellings marks their village

(above, left). Two founding members occupy th
courtyard—a man sitting at right, his mant
about him, and a priestess in the customary
kneeling posture. A glyph behind her head
name: Chimalma, or Reposing Shield.
     The migration begins with a paddle across t
the year 1 Flint Knife (corresponding to AI
noted by the square-framed glyph above the f
that track the migration. The first stop is a vi

god who was all-important in the Aztec pantheon, Huitzilopochtli, ensconced in a leafy bower within Colhuacan, "curved mountain." The god, whose name means "hummingbird left," peers out from a stylized hummingbird's beak. He speaks, as is indicated by the squiggles floating above his head, commanding the migrants to move on. And so they do, along with eight other tribes, each of which is represented by a male figure seen in front of a house and is identified by a

tribal glyph *(above)*. The first glyph, for example, depicts a fishnet, because the tribe was known as the People of the Net, the Matlatzinca.

Leading the trek are four *teomama,* or god bearers, noted for their piety. Effigies of the deities are contained in sacred bundles carried on their backs. Tezcacoatl, Mirror Snake, strides ahead of the procession with the precious image of Huitzilopochtli, as Reposing Shield brings up the rear.

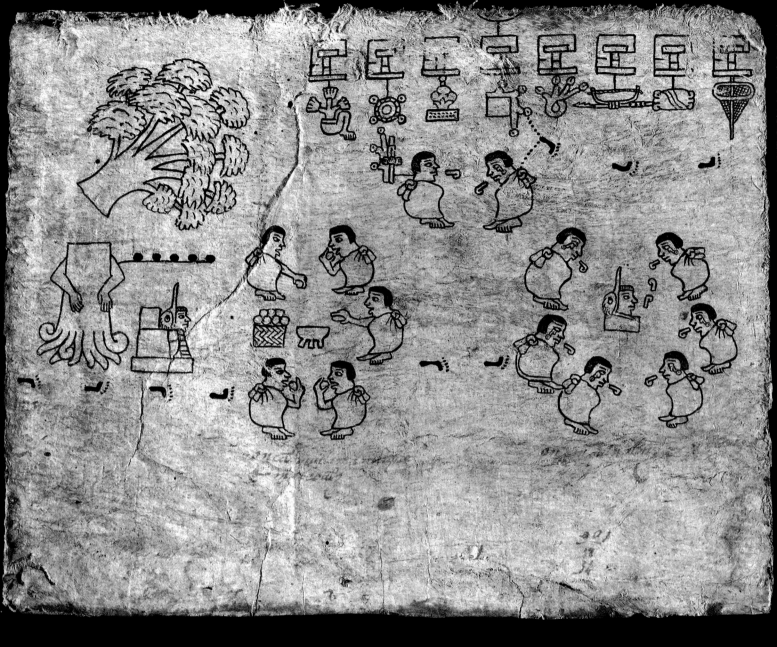

Not far into the journey, the wanderers come upon a region of idyllic beauty and fruitfulness, shaded by an enormous, anthropomorphized tree. They erect an altar dedicated to Huitzilopochtli and celebrate with a feast. Then misfortune strikes: As they sit eating, the tree breaks in two *(above)*, an omen of the worst imaginable kind, associated in Aztec legend with the loss of paradise.

Knowledge of the event that caused the tree to split

has been lost to time. No doubt an Aztec narrator, interpreting the codex for his audience, would have filled in the details from memory. In any case, the outcome is graphically clear. Huitzilopochtli exhorts the tribesmen gathered in a circle to resume their wanderings. They weep at the thought of leaving behind the eight other tribes.

The migrants start out, following the god bearers and pausing from time to time along the way to hunt

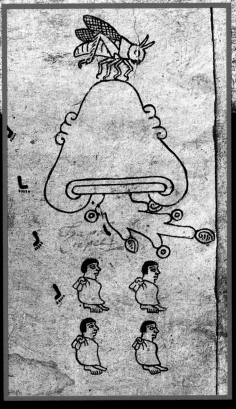

and to sacrifice victims captured in skirmishes. Their trek will continue for many generations; the full codex shows 22 successive stopovers. Finally the nomads reach the shores of Lake Tetzcoco. They settle at Chapultepec—"grasshopper hill"—on the lake's west bank, where a freshwater spring *(right)* gushes from the bedrock. And here they will remain—until dislodged by the intertribal conflicts that perpetually trouble this second promised land.

The rise of Tenochtitlan, in symbolic overview, adorns the frontispiece of the Codex Mendoza. The founding fathers pay homage to the city's eagle-crowned emblem, positioned above the Aztec heraldic shield. The crossed blue bands represent the canals that divided the city into quadrants. In the bottom panel, burning temples mark two early victories over rival city-states, Colhuacan and Tenayuca, won while the Aztecs served as mercenaries to the Tepanecs.

Two House, marked by two dots, is the founding year of Tenochtitlan, AD 1325.

Three Rabbit stands for the city's second year and is marked by three dots.

Four Reed represents Tenochtitlan's third year, indicated by four dots.

Five Flint Knife, the fourth year of the island city's existence, has five dots.

THE BEGINNINGS OF EMPIRE AT TENOCHTITLAN

In their new home of Chapultepec, the Aztecs become vassals of the Colhuacans and serve them as mercenaries. But, beginning to resent their status and growing ever more powerful, they provoke the wrath of the Colhuacan leaders. Forced to flee for their lives, they fade into Lake Tetzcoco's swamps. In these soggy premises they found their imperial city, Tenochtitlan, on the site foretold by Huitzilopochtli—a rock from which a cactus sprouted, with an eagle perched among the thorns. Thus the city's name: Tenochtitlan, or "place of the prickly pear cactus," and also its imperial emblem. (The same configuration appears on the flag of modern Mexico—only today a snake dangles from the bird's beak.)

The eagle and cactus also emblazon the frontispiece of the Codex Mendoza *(opposite)*. Among the most magnificent of all surviving codices, this document relates the Aztec story year by year in 16 brilliantly detailed pages, from the city's inception in 1325 until the time of the Spanish conquest. Probably commissioned by the first viceroy of New Spain, Don Antonio de Mendoza, after whom it is named, it chronicles the reign of each Aztec ruler, starting with the city's traditional founder, the priest Tenoch, and the nine leaders of the Aztecs, and ending with Motecuhzoma II. Each date, place, and character is carefully recorded, every conquest proudly depicted. For the benefit of the codex's Spanish readers, the story was rendered in Spanish directly on the pages.

Around the edges of the frontispiece run glyphs for calendar years. The four signs shown enlarged at left were basic to the system and were repeated in sequence every four years, with dots from 1 to 13 representing the actual years. Every 52 years a "century" was turned. The first year of the new century was always designated 2 Reed. It was ushered in with the extinguishment of the old ceremonial fires and the lighting of new ones—represented by the fire-making device seen opposite in the glyph at the bottom of the page, third symbol from the right.

A stone-and-cactus name glyph means Tenoch, the capital's principal founder.

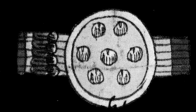

A sheaf of spears and a shield with tufts of eagle down signify Aztec power.

A burning, ruined temple is the glyph for conquest.

A walled hill identifies the city of Tenayuca, the "place with walls."

reer of the Aztecs' first hereditary monarch,
who became ruler in 1376 and reigned for 21
years, as is revealed by the marginal date
glyphs. His name, Acamapichtli—Hand Grasp-
ing Arrow-Canes—is depicted by his personal
glyph, seen behind his head. During his reign
he captured four towns, symbolized by their rulers' heads. His last conquest—Xochimilco, or
Flowers on Arable Soil—paid rich tribute.

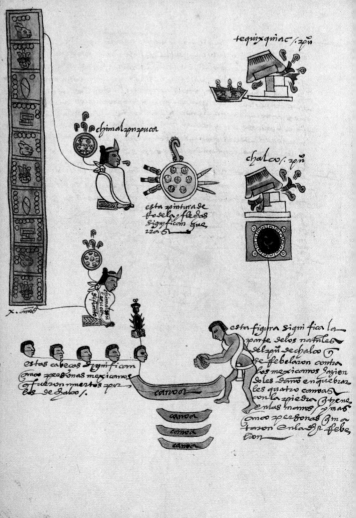

Traced here is the troubled reign of Tenochtitlan's third ruler, Chimalpopoca, or Smoking
Shield, which was marred by defeat. During his
assault on a place called Chalco, the defenders
sank four Aztec war canoes; they also slew numerous Aztec warriors, as is represented by the
five severed heads. Chimalpopoca, who was executed by the Tepanecs, is shown alive, then with
body slumped forward, voice stilled. His death

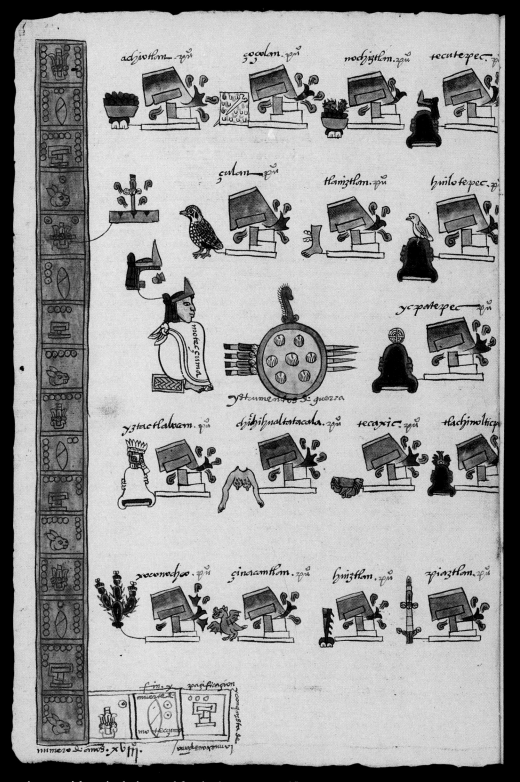

A page with an inglorious end for the Aztecs examines the reign of Motecuhzoma II, who rang up impressive victories—as befitted his name, Angry Lord. His triumphs yielded not only much tribute but also many captives for sacrifice on Tenochtitlan's altars. The trio of year glyphs added to the bottom of the page dates the Spaniards' arrival in Mexico, Motecuhzoma's death, and the founding of New Spain upon the ruins of the Aztec empire.

PEOPLE IN SEARCH OF A PAST

he villagers of Coatlinchan, near the immense ghost city of Teotihuacan, were distraught. The designers of the National Museum of Anthropology in Mexico City had decided in 1964 to grace the museum entrance with a monumental carving that was thought to represent Tlaloc, the rain god. The enormous statue lay on its side just as its sculptors had left it more than a thousand years earlier. If the god were moved, the rains, and therefore life itself, might cease.

Not until government officials promised to shower Coatlinchan with a variety of beneficial public works did the villagers relent. A special trailer with dozens of rubber tires was brought from Texas to transport the 168-ton basalt idol. In a last, desperate bid to keep their rain god at home, the alarmed villagers sabotaged the vehicle. In the end, however, secular authority prevailed, and the statue was taken to its place of honor in Mexico City. Thousands lined the roadways to watch the great stone image of Mexico's oldest prehistoric divinity pass by.

And then a remarkable thing happened. It *poured*. Even though the wet and dry seasons are well defined in the Valley of Mexico and every onlooker knew that the time of year was wrong for rain, it fell in torrents along the route. Nor was this just a sudden shower: In defiance of the calendar, the downpour continued

Fashioned from clay and bits of mother-of-pearl by a 10th-century Toltec Indian craftsman, a bearded head peers from a coyote's jaws. Works like this convinced the Aztecs that the Toltecs, whose heritage they claimed for themselves, had been divine artisans.

through the night. "People joked about the coincidence," recalled the Mexican author Victor Alba, "but later, as Tlaloc was being set in place in the museum garden, rain poured down each time he was moved, and the Mexicans began to feel an astonishment not far from superstitious awe."

Happily, the succeeding years have brought no untimely drought to Coatlinchan, and its villagers have received the rewards the government promised them: a school, a medical clinic, a new road, and electric power. The story of the statue's rain-drenched journey survives, however, as something more than an entertaining anecdote because of what it suggests about the Mexican people and their heritage.

In Mexico, ancient roots and antecedents still matter; although the country is Roman Catholic, pagan memories intertwine. Few if any of the awed spectators who came to see Tlaloc actually considered him sacred, but in their eyes he possessed a complex emotional significance far beyond that of an antique hunk of carved rock. It is especially ironic to consider that the skirted figure may not have been Tlaloc after all, as scholars now have reason to believe, but his sister or another female deity. What was important was that the villagers had no doubt whatsoever it was Tlaloc.

Tlaloc was not originally an Aztec god, but rather one of scores that the Aztecs adopted from earlier cultures. Such wholesale cultural borrowing did not bother the Aztecs, nor does it deter modern Mexicans in their deep and sentimental identification with

Inhabitants of Coatlinchan run along the road outside their town in April 1964 as the supposed effigy of the rain god, Tlaloc, begins its 30-mile journey to the Museum of Anthropology in Mexico City. The 168-ton idol had been taken from a nearby streambed, where it had lain undisturbed for more than a thousand years.

the civilizations that ruled their land before the coming of the Spaniards. The Aztecs created fabulous myths about their precursors, and their descendants tend to accept them whole, in spite of what archaeologists might tell them to the contrary.

The ascent of the nomadic Aztecs to power in the Valley of Mexico left them with a need to establish not only noble ancestry but also the imprimatur of destiny. Other tribes were hardly impressed with the claims of these miserable wanderers to be the chosen rulers of the valley and its peoples. After all, less than 200 years before the conquistadors marched in with stamping horses and roaring cannons, the dusty, snake-eating Aztecs were living in earthen hovels on an unpromising island in Lake Tetzcoco. Among the more than 50 Indian groups that contended for domination of the area in the 13th century, the Aztecs stood out only for their talent for mayhem and slaughter—and for this they were often hired as mercenaries.

Desperate for legitimacy, the Aztecs set about with single-minded fervor to establish it. Perhaps their most dramatic act was to import a prolific breeder with a good pedigree. They brought in a Colhuacan prince who claimed descent from the reputedly noble Toltecs and arranged for him to marry no fewer than 20 Aztec women, who presumably would then bear him numerous blue-blooded children. Aristocracy on command. It worked. Itzcoatl, one of the sons of the prince, led his men into a major battle and brought home much plunder and many captives. Not content with creating a new national ethos, Itzcoatl set out to obliterate the old. He destroyed tribal records that might have cast doubt on the nobility of the Aztecs' past and the preordained, godsent brilliance of their future. A new, glorious, and thoroughly slanted history emerged.

Itzcoatl and his successor, the first Motecuhzoma, enlisted allies and expanded violently and dramatically all over the valley. The resulting tribute, wrung from conquered peoples, formed the basis for the unspeakably opulent city of Tenochtitlan. But rule though they did over the lives and fortunes of the conquered, the Aztecs could not erase the truth of their abject beginnings. The subject peoples must have realized that their own purchase of the Aztecs' martial skills had given the ambitious mercenaries the wherewithal to scrabble upward. The former lords, now vassals, had clasped the Aztec viper to their breasts. Its fangs went straight into their hearts.

47

According to the Aztecs' own self-serving codices, their migration began about AD 1100, swirling out from an ancestral homeland called Aztlan, "place of the herons." Of Aztlan's true location nothing is known except that it lay northwest of Mexico City; perhaps it was as far away as the southwestern United States, perhaps as close as 60 miles to Tenochtitlan, their capital.

A less promising troupe of migrants can scarcely be imagined. Guided by Huitzilopochtli, a ferocious deity who in the course of time had evolved from an earth-god of fertility into a symbol of militarism and imperialism associated with the sun, they ate vermin, stole women, and took captives for human sacrifices to placate their god. The sun would not rise, they believed, unless Huitzilopochtli was nourished with hearts cut from the bodies of living men.

The Aztecs' wanderings would come to an end, declared their god through the mouths of his priests, only when they arrived at the site that he had chosen at the start of time to be their capital. According to an Aztec chronicle, they would know this place by a sign:

THE STERN ART OF A MILITARISTIC PEOPLE

Taking his lead from the Aztecs, who appropriated the heritage of their predecessors, the Toltecs, the Spanish friar Sahagún extolled the Toltecs as the master craftsmen of Mesoamerica. "All that now exists, is their discovery," he wrote. Yet for the most part these militaristic people exhibited neither the artistic skills nor the aesthetic sensibilities of their own predecessors, the Olmecs and the Teotihuacanos. But although Toltec art is often crude and relies on bellicose themes, qualities exemplified in the three-foot-tall stone warrior at right, it also includes well-finished ceramic pieces. Among them are the coiled serpent pectoral below and the animal effigy at left, which combines human and supernatural characteristics.

where the resting eagle "screams and spreads its wings and eats, and the serpent is torn apart."

Wherever the Aztecs went they were rejected as vile and barbaric by the sedentary peoples they encountered. By 1168 they had reached the Valley of Mexico, skulking on its fringes. Feared by all, they trudged from place to place. Twice in 20 years they occupied the strategic hilltop heights of Chapultepec beside Lake Tetzcoco, and twice their indignant neighbors threw them out.

By 1319, weary and discouraged, seemingly farther than ever from Huitzilopochtli's promise of riches and supremacy, they straggled into noble Colhuacan and sought asylum. The Colhua, needing mercenaries and fully aware of their uninvited guests' talent for slaughter, decided to keep the Aztecs usefully at hand. With what surely must have been a cruel snicker, they offered the coarse suppliants refuge at a nearby place called Tizapan, a bare patch of volcanic rock infested with snakes. To their surprise the Aztecs not only survived but also thrived. As one chronicle describes it, they "rejoiced greatly as soon as they saw the snakes, and they roasted and cooked them all and ate them all up." Impressed by such resilience, Achitometl, the ruler of Colhuacan, and other leaders of Colhuacan put them to work as warriors, and thus the Aztecs won the confidence of their hosts.

But soon Huitzilopochtli came among them and said: "Hear me, we will not remain here but go where we shall find those whom we shall capture and dominate. But we will not make the mistake of being nice to the Colhuacans. We will begin a war. I order this: Go and ask Achitometl for his offspring, his virgin daughter, his own dearly loved child; I know, and I shall give her to you."

The Aztecs went to the ruler as commanded and asked for his daughter to be their god's bride. He consented, and they took her back to Tizapan, where Huitzilopochtli appeared again to them and said: "Kill and skin the daughter of Achitometl, I order you, and when you have skinned her, dress some priest in her skin. Then go call on Achitometl."

They did so, and Achitometl accepted their invitation to attend the consecration of his daughter as a goddess. Entering the darkened temple, he placed gifts of blood and flowers at the feet of the idol there. Then he offered incense. "This began to burn," according to the chronicles, "and the room lighted up with the fire. Thus the king suddenly perceived the priest who was seated next to

49

the idol, and saw that he was dressed in his daughter's skin. The king was filled with a wild terror."

In rage the Colhua banished the Aztecs to the swamps of Lake Tetzcoco. One can picture them milling aimlessly across the soggy ground, bitter and confused, led to this hopeless desolation by the elusive promises of their god. And then on a low island surrounded by reeds they noticed an eagle resting on a prickly pear. As they watched, the eagle spread its wings and screamed in triumph, the god-given sign. Their journey had ended, and their bloodthirsty spread across the Valley of Mexico was about to begin. They would build an empire based largely on an enthusiastic dedication to war.

The inventive Aztecs, newly rich and climbing fast, partly satisfied their yearning for legitimacy by associating themselves with peoples of the past. It was the more recent Toltecs that most impressed them with their supposed achievements, and whom they sought to emulate. Little did it matter that the Aztecs had got them completely wrong—only within recent years has archaeology revealed the full degree to which the Toltecs' admirers were misinformed about them.

Further back in time were the builders of Teotihuacan, of whom so little was known that the Aztecs could make up anything they wanted, with no one to say them nay. In any case, they were sufficiently awed by the Teotihuacanos' ruined city—which had been even bigger and more magnificent than their own capital of Tenochtitlan—to believe that it was the birthplace of the gods and to hold some of their religious ceremonies there on a regular basis. Here again the truth about the site and the people who inhabited it would have to wait for archaeology to shed light on the Teotihuacanos and their truly remarkable achievements.

Even more remote in time were the Olmecs, relics of whose glorious past have been dug up in Tenochtitlan, evidence of how much the Aztec upstarts revered these mysterious people of the coastal lowlands. Certainly the Aztecs owed them a large debt: Perhaps without even knowing it, they absorbed from the Olmec heritage the basis of their calendar, their glyph system, and their love of monumental sculpture and architecture.

The Olmecs were an amazing people, but for a long time they went unrecognized for their seminal role in the development of

Mesoamerican culture. It was thought by anthropologists that the Maya were the parent culture of the Gulf Coast lowlands in ancient times. The realization that the Olmecs in fact preceded them would come slowly and reluctantly to the world at large. The first of the monumental Olmec sculptures to be discovered was the head dug up in 1862 at Tres Zapotes in the region southeast of Veracruz. The sugarcane workers who found it buried in the earth supposed it at first to be an inverted iron kettle. But then the face came to light: round, powerful, with thick lips and nose, it was plain to all who beheld it that this was a special work indeed. Yet

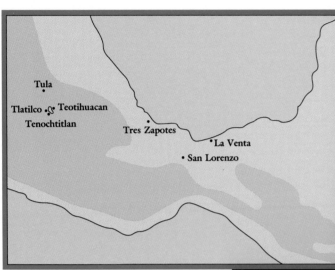

Olmec civilization flourished from 1200 to 400 BC on Mexico's humid, sweltering Gulf Coast plain. There lay the great population centers Tres Zapotes, San Lorenzo, and La Venta, where this eight-foot-high basalt head, thought to be the portrait of a king, was found.

51

THE OLMECS' BRILLIANT SCULPTURAL OUTPOURING

Founders of Mesoamerica's first civilization, the Olmecs were also Mexico's first master sculptors. Using only simple tools, such as adzes made of hard rock, and hollow bamboo drills, they carved volcanic basalt into huge monuments, including colossal portrait heads and altars, and turned still-more-resistant stone into highly polished miniature works of art. Indeed, so assured was the Olmec artists' command over their materials that even small works, like the adz head at top right, one of thousands of such ceremonial items to survive, conveys a sense of monumentality.

Characterizing much Olmec sculpture is a trait scholars refer to as the were-jaguar baby face, as seen in the puffy figure at right. Half-animal, half-human, such a visage suggests the Olmecs' spiritual kinship with the jaguar, lord of the jungle. In many such pieces the head also displays a deep V-shaped cleft, possibly inspired by a similar groove found in crocodiles and toads, which the Olmecs apparently regarded as manifestations of the earth mother in animal form.

The face of a were-jaguar, a creature of Olmec mythology, decorates a jade adz that was used in rituals.

Carved from gray basalt, this seated figure, perhaps a wrestler, measures just a little over two feet high.

Babylike in appearance, a hollow ceramic figure has the stubby arms common to many Olmec works.

for years, it—along with other examples of Olmec artistry—remained in a kind of cultural vacuum. Not until the 1930s would the Olmecs be recognized as Mesoamerica's earliest civilization. The moment of truth came on January 16, 1939, when the American archaeologist Matthew W. Stirling discovered at Tres Zapotes a carved stone bearing a Maya-type date on one side and a typically Olmec feline face on the other. This might have been considered a fairly inconsequential find had it not been dated 31 BC, making it centuries older than any known Maya object.

With the discovery of more and more Olmec objects, a persistent question arose—why had so many of them been defaced and buried? The obvious and long-held inference was that these had been smashed by hostile invaders—or, perhaps, by the Olmecs themselves in a desperate effort to keep them from desecration by their enemies. However, in 1966, when another American archaeologist, Michael Coe, excavated an Olmec site at San Lorenzo, southeast of Tres Zapotes, he found that the great stone sculptures he unearthed—heads, a kneeling man, and a jaguar figure—had been systematically mutilated and then buried along certain fixed alignments. The only plausible explanation, Coe concluded, was that a deliberate, ritualistic burial of the sculptures had taken place, something possible only as part of a formal ceremony and not as a frantic response to attack.

Many other tantalizing mysteries associated with the Olmecs may be beyond solving. But with their ultimate demise, which itself is a mystery, other peoples came foward. Slowly during the centuries after 1000 BC the increasing population of the Valley of Mexico began to coalesce at Cuicuilco, in an area now within the urban limits of Mexico City, and at Teotihuacan, located in a lesser side valley 33 miles to the northeast. When volcanic eruptions destroyed Cuicuilco, the way was clear for Teotihuacan to grow unchallenged. And grow it did, expanding steadily from a village into a carefully planned city larger in area than its mighty contemporary, imperial Rome. By AD 500, Teotihuacan had a population of at least 125,000—perhaps as many as 200,000—and covered eight square miles. In the scale of its conception and in the monumental grandeur of its buildings, nothing like it existed before or after in the pre-Columbian New World. But why the city was abandoned and what happened to its people are as much an enigma as the fate of the Olmecs.

Although Teotihuacan means "city of the gods," there is less to the name than meets the eye. It is simply a label applied to the overgrown site long afterward by the admiring Aztecs, who sensed even among the desolation of its ruins some lingering presence of the divine, as if only the gods could have dwelled here. No one knows what Teotihuacan was called in its heyday; no one knows what the Teotihuacanos called themselves. Not until the past hundred years have archaeologists been able to sketch, however roughly, the outlines of its rise and fall.

Visitors who made the mule trek out from Mexico City to inspect the site in the 19th century found a rumpled landscape dotted with earthen mounds, the largest of which, called the Pyramid of the Sun, was ascended by a zigzag path leading to its 210-foot-high top. Giant maguey plants, some as large as 20 feet across, thrived among the tangles of lesser vegetation. Here and there a brick or stone protruded, tantalizing evidence that something monumental lay beneath it all.

The silence and torpor gave little clue that Teotihuacan had once been a crowded metropolis, the most important marketplace and religious center in Mesoamerica. It had been a city of colors, ablaze with fresh paint and sparkling with reflected light, richly decorated with murals and frescoes. At its peak, Teotithuacan held sway over an area of some 10,000 square miles, a region about the size of the Netherlands today.

The city's very location was inspired. Teotihuacan lay close to sources of obsidian, the volcanic glass that was indispensable for sharp-edged tools in a society that never mastered iron or bronze. It was watered by springs, making irrigation possible. Physically it lay squarely astride the narrow, mountain-hemmed route between the highland valleys and the Gulf Coast, ensuring not only wide markets but also subtle power over trade. And emotionally it seems to have been infused with a profound religious significance, reinforcing its economic supremacy with the magnetism of a goal of pilgrimages. Even the humblest Teotihuacan dwellings had altars to their gods.

By AD 100, Teotihuacan had about 60,000 people and covered more than two square miles. Sometime between the birth of Christ and AD 150, two great truncated pyramids—known

HOUSEHOLD GRAVES OF TLATILCO

In 1936, brickworkers digging for clay in a Mexico City suburb stumbled upon a pre-Columbian site that would yield, over the course of two decades, hundreds of graves containing skeletons and dozens of small terra-cotta vessels and figurines (below). These were the ghostly reminders of a large village whose inhabitants buried their dead beneath their homes, laying successive generations to rest on top of one another. The village dated from

around 1200 BC, when the Olmecs ruled the Gulf Coast 200 miles to the east. Moreover, some of the objects, such as the Olmec-style acrobat at lower right, had apparently been brought to the village as part of a lively trade in goods and ideas.

Although the residents of Tlatilco may have conducted business with the Olmecs, only a small percentage of their grave goods are Olmec. The Tlatilcoans, in fact, had a distinctive art style of their own, dominated by female imagery that some scholars connect with earth goddesses and the cultivation of the Indian staple, corn. The curious double-headed figurine at right may be a personification of rare joined, or double, ears that occasionally sprout on plants.

today as the Pyramid of the Sun and the Pyramid of the Moon—were erected, and the main axis of the city, the so-called Avenue of the Dead, was extended to more than three miles in length. A huge rectangular mound known as the Citadel was also built, measuring more than 1,650 feet along its longer sides. It comprised four embankments, each about 19 feet high and 260 feet thick, and may have served as a housing area for priests or public officials, as well as a ceremonial center. Fifteen pyramids crowned the immense structure.

Although it is not clear whether the evolution of Teotihuacan followed a master plan established early in the city's history, the resulting size and scale appear to be the result of some sort of overall scheme. Two grand avenues bisected it, and Teotihuacan's huge public compounds and numerous temples were laid out along them in repetitive fashion on a scale so vast that the grand buildings at one end of the city were scarcely visible from the other.

As the culture and influence of Teotihuacan expanded southward in the fifth century, residents of surrounding areas relocated within the city or became dependent on it, a development that prevented the growth of rival centers. But, then, quite suddenly, a violent, fiery catastrophe overtook it about AD 750. Even after much of its center was destroyed, Teotihuacan's humbled remnants still constituted the largest community in central Mexico. By 850, Toltec tribes had drifted in to occupy the site, but what eventually became of them is lost to history. Knowing nothing of Teotihuacan's development, the Aztecs assumed that the earthen mounds they saw were Toltec. They erred by hundreds of years and an entire civilization.

This same firm belief in the Toltec origins of Teotihuacan persisted among the 19th-century visitors who came to view the mysterious ruins. One of these was Désiré Charnay, a brash young Frenchman whose energies seem to have been more or less evenly divided between archaeological speculation and Mexican women, whom he found irresistible. His fascination with Mesoamerican ruins eventually brought him, in 1882, to the enigmatic hill called the Pyramid of the Sun, which he promptly climbed.

"The ascent was arduous, especially with a burning sun beating down on us," he wrote years later in his memoirs. "But when we reached the top, we were amply repaid by the glorious view that unfolded before our enraptured gaze. To the north the Pyramid of the Moon, and the great Avenue of the Dead with its tombs and tumuluses, covering a space of nine square miles; to the south and southwest the hills of Tlaxcala, the villages of San Martin and San Juan, the snowy top of Iztaccihuatl towering above the Matlacinga range; and in the west the Valley of Mexico with its lakes."

Charnay's curiosity resulted in the first tentative diggings at the site. He delighted not only in huge monuments but also in small discoveries that cast some light on the lives of these long-vanished peoples. He was aided in a couple of instances by a most curious ally—ants. One day when he was working at the Pyramid of the Moon, he found in the course of his excavations "numerous pieces of

Official protector of Mexico's monuments, the self-taught archaeologist Leopoldo Batres pioneered—albeit recklessly—excavations at Teotihuacan, seen above in an 1895 photo. His initial exploration began with a search for gold; by 1905, he had mule trains hauling out dirt by the ton.

worked obsidian, precious stones, beads, and the like, within the circuit of ants' nests, which these busy insects had extracted from the ground in digging their galleries; and now on the summit of the lesser pyramid, I again came upon my friends, and among the things I picked out of their nests was a perfect earring of obsidian, very small and as thin as a sheet of paper."

Although Charnay's work was widely ignored at the time, it did pique the curiosity of one man in a position to do something about it: Leopoldo Batres. The flamboyantly mustached Batres was the illegitimate elder half-brother of the wife of Porfirio Díaz, Mexico's dictator-president. He persuaded Díaz to appoint him inspector and protector of the archaeological monuments of Mexico. The exalted title gave him the right to excavate anywhere in the country even though, as a subsequent Mexican archaeologist has said, Batres "had no knowledge whatever of digging techniques or of serious study methods." In 1884 he began to poke among the enormous pyramids that he, like everyone else, considered "our most ancient records of the Toltec race." His excavations were earnest but unprofessional. Working from an enormous budget while many Mexicans barely had enough to eat, he unearthed temples, windowless dwellings, skeletons, and more murals. Roaming beyond the pyramids he began to sense the vast dimensions of the city and the care with which it had been built; every surface had been carefully paved with mortar and small stones. Finding no fortifications or armaments, he assumed Teotihuacan had been a peaceful, open city. All these indications of the city's life paled, however, beside the stunning evidence of its death: Almost everywhere Batres looked, he found unmistakable traces of an all-consuming fire.

Finding that not even his huge budget was enough for the task, Batres turned his attentions elsewhere in 1886. The unprotected ruins fell victim to a dreamer named Antonio García Cubas, an engineer by profession. Convinced that the pyramids contained hidden chambers like those of the Great Pyramid in Egypt, García Cubas chopped a hole several thousand cubic yards in size into the Pyramid of the Moon before conceding he was wrong.

Batres returned to Teotihuacan in 1905, determined to excavate the entire 738-foot-square, 20-story-high Pyramid of the Sun in time for the centennial of Mexican independence in 1910. The date usefully coincided with the 80th birthday of President Díaz and thereby seemed to assure the necessary supply of funds. Indeed, as the author Brian Fagan has calculated it, Batres's second season of excavations "used up more money than the entire social welfare budget for Mexico." His workers began removing dirt at the rate of 100 tons an hour, 1,000 tons a day, carting away the debris on a railroad built especially to serve the site. Even then, progress was slow. In retrospect, this prodigious effort gives eloquent proof of the antiquity of Teotihuacan. The drifting dust of Mexico had fallen lightly, grain by grain, onto the abandoned platforms and staircases of the great pyramid. Then seeds drifted in, and plants took root. The plants grew, decayed, and new plants replaced them, only to decay in their turn. Day after day, year after year, century after century, the vegetation rotted until the accumulated earth lay packed so deep that even battalions of men with machines could scarcely take it all away. The greatest building in Mesoamerica had become a hill.

Batres's excavations soon encountered serious problems. When rains came, the clay-based material between the bricks on the surface of the excavated pyramid began to dissolve, threatening to let the whole exterior slide off. Batres hurriedly installed wooden chutes to deflect the rain and hired a team of masons to replace the clay with reinforced mortar of lime, cement, and volcanic rock. Advancing from brick to brick, using small spoons, they scraped deep into the joints and replaced the clay with mortar. The structure was saved.

As the excavations continued, Batres found polychrome frescoes on the pyramid's surfaces and clay figures and ornaments at its highest level, along with remnants of child sacrifice at each corner. He discovered the debris of pottery, ceramics, sculpture, and, nearby, a group of dwellings, richly decorated with carvings and frescoes, that he called the House of the Priests. All this suggested how much more must lay hidden in what Batres termed "one of the most interesting cities in the world of archaeology." But despite such a claim and the vigorous ascent of the partly excavated pyramid by the 76-year-old Díaz himself in 1906, the resources Batres thought necessary to finish the work were not forthcoming, and he resigned. When President Díaz was overthrown five years later, Batres fled to Paris to join him in exile.

Although professional archaeologists lamented Batres's heavy-handed methods, the evidence he unearthed of Teotihuacan's past glories whetted their appetite for more. Work resumed in 1917 under the direction of Manuel Gamio, a Mexican archaeologist with a doctorate from Columbia University in New York. Setting aside his duties as head of the department of anthropology at the National Museum in Mexico City, Gamio focused his efforts near Teotihuacan's Citadel. There he soon uncovered the dazzling Feathered Serpent Temple, with its decoration of serpent heads and goggle-eyed faces thought to represent Tlaloc. Archaeology at Teotihuacan was becoming more methodical and scholarly. The Swedes (rare in being able to afford the luxury of archaeology during the Great Depression of the 1930s) sent Sigvald Linné, who in the course of several expeditions became one of Europe's foremost authorities on Mexican antiquities. Finding a multitude of varied houses and many narrow streets, Linné proved that Teotihuacan had been far more than just a ceremonial center, as his predecessors had supposed. Other diggers uncovered brilliant frescoes and a 5,000-square-yard palace.

But as late as 1960 the major mysteries surrounding Teotihuacan remained unsolved: Why was it built and what happened to it in the end? Then, like the petals of a flower rapidly unfolding in time-lapse photography, the layers concealing Teotihuacan were at last peeled back to expose, within a few short years, much of the grandeur that had only been guessed at. And with discovery came revelation.

Supported by a large appropriation from a new Mexican government, the archaeologist Jorge Acosta, one of the assistants of Ignacio Bernal, the overall project director, completed excavations of the area around the 152-foot-high Pyramid of the Moon, the Avenue of the Dead, and part of the plaza in front of the Pyramid of the Sun. Later, Bernal joined Acosta to restore the Pyramid of the Moon—a task made more historically accurate by the discovery of one cornerstone in its original position. This enabled Acosta and his team to

Dapper Manuel Gamio, head of the Mexican government's Department of Archaeology and Anthropology, embarked on a painstaking excavation of Teotihuacan's Citadel in 1917. Beneath a mound of earth, he discovered the Feathered Serpent Temple (below), *a seven-tiered pyramid that originally rose 65 feet.*

reconstruct the angle of ascent and replace in their correct positions 565 original staircase stones that over the years had fallen from the pyramid and tumbled into the plaza.

Throughout the site, Acosta and Bernal tore down what they considered inferior structures dating from late in Teotihuacan's history in order to reveal the classic buildings that stood beneath them. Along the majestic length of the Avenue of the Dead, the great city lay at last partly revealed in its essentials.

Complementing the Mexican scientists' efforts was the painstaking work of René Millon, an archaeologist from the University of Rochester. Convinced that Teotihuacan was even larger and more complex than anyone had yet shown, Millon decided to dedicate his life to solving its mysteries. He devised a plan to photograph it from the air, explore it thoroughly on foot, do spot excavations, and then compare the aerial pictures with information gathered on the ground. The air surveys were carried out in 1962 and covered an area of 22 square miles, of which 12½ proved to be within Teotihuacan. The mapping took five more years to finish.

The results were impressive. More than 2,200 one-story apartment compounds had existed within Teotihuacan's boundaries. "Each patio admitted light and air to the surrounding apartments," Millon reported. "Each made it possible for the residents to be out-of-doors yet alone." The city was filled with several hundred workshops, almost 400 for obsidian alone, suggesting that it buzzed with intensive craft activity. A separate precinct inhabited by immigrant craftsmen from Oaxaca, 200 miles southeast of Teotihuacan, was deduced from traces of pottery and tomb decorations, giving clear evidence of faraway political and commercial liaisons. And though Teotihuacan was not enclosed by walls, it was far from the defenseless open city Batres and others had imagined it to be. Its apartment compounds and narrow streets and the natural barriers of spiny nopal cactus in the surrounding countryside may well have served to impede attackers.

Even after Millon's thoroughgoing study, other astonishing discoveries lay ahead. In 1971, a hard rain caused a depression to form at the foot of the Pyramid of the Sun. Digging there disclosed the remains of an ancient stairway that led beneath the pyramid into a 112-yard-long tunnel. When investigators explored it they encoun-

THE LOOTED MURALS OF TEOTIHUACAN

In 1976, San Francisco's M. H. de Young Museum received word of an unexpected bequest. The curator sent to investigate was dumbstruck at what he found. In the benefactor's house, "on the floor, tables and walls, glued to pieces of plywood, in cardboard boxes"

A conservator (above) works to restore a mural fragment. The process involves both stabilizing the deteriorating adobe backing and reassembling scattered pieces such as those at right, which come from a frieze of a serpent and trees.

were more than 70 priceless mural fragments from Teotihuacan.

Harald Wagner, the deceased collector, had acquired the treasure in the mid-1960s after the Mexican government expanded Teotihuacan's archaeological zone. Looters posing as uprooted farmers scavenging household building materials dug randomly into the ruins and gouged out large chunks of the colorfully decorated walls.

The frescoes found few buyers. Liable to immediate confiscation if discovered, the fragments were also fragile and unappealingly dirty and unwieldy. A few went to museums; others were hawked in village markets or allowed to crumble to dust. Wagner, whose passion was architectural restoration, somehow managed to acquire the pieces he ultimately willed to the museum. In 1986, to resolve the ethical dilemma his bequest posed, that institution returned most of them to Mexico.

tered a series of 29 masonry walls blocking the way, each plainly built by someone who could only have been working outward. At the end, almost directly beneath the pyramid's center, was a large cave. Out from it branched four smaller chambers, and the whole had been enlarged to the shape of a cloverleaf.

Scholars have argued persuasively that the cave, formed by an enormous bubble of gas in lava streaming from deep within the earth, was the very reason the Pyramid of the Sun was built where it was. Since the pyramid was the first major building in all of Teotihuacan, it follows that the city itself was founded because of—not merely over—a cave. To understand this extraordinary conclusion, it is necessary to know that caves had tremendous symbolic importance in ancient Mexico. Codices and glyphs abound with images of caves, and therefore of creation, of the womb, of life itself, of the origin of the sun and the moon. In this arid land, springs were sacred, and they often bubbled forth in caves, originating, it was thought, from deep in the underworld to which the dead journeyed. The big grotto at Teotihuacan, though dry now, apparently once had abundant water. Even the great god Tlaloc figures in the mysticism associated with caves, for he ruled not only the rains but also caverns and rivers. The cave beneath Teotihuacan's Pyramid of the Sun may have been the focal shrine of a cult, whose members, perhaps, were the city's founding fathers. Furthermore, there is abundant evidence of continued use of the caves in the early centuries after the pyramid's construction.

But having so long prospered, why then did Teotihuacan collapse, and what did the burn marks on so many of its ruins have to say about its end? Climatologists have searched for the cause of Teotihuacan's death in an environmental crisis, perhaps erosion and crop failure or prolonged drought. Huge quantities of wood were burned as fuel to make the quicklime on which Teotihuacan's construction depended, and over time massive tree felling could have denuded the countryside for miles around. The climate may gradually have become drier. But disturbance of the ecology was unlikely to have been the only cause; and whatever the

terminal crisis, Millon suggested that the city's leadership may have lacked the flexibility and imagination to deal with it. Perhaps, under profound stress, Teotihuacan's distinctive residential patterns were its undoing. Its crowded apartment compounds, separated by high walls and segregated by class and social status, may have fostered a civic morale too brittle to cope with hard times.

One of the intriguing aspects of the fire that accompanied the city's demise is the archaeological evidence of its confinement largely to religious structures, particularly along the Avenue of the Dead, where more than 100 temples and shrines stood. All told, some 600 buildings were put to the torch. Millon and other scholars argue that the burning was carried out "through a coordinated series of planned

The stepped shape of Teotihuacan's Pyramid of the Moon comes gradually to light during excavations conducted in the 1960s by the Mexican archaeologists Jorge Acosta and Ignacio Bernal. More than 600 workmen labored to clear and restore the imposing 152-foot-high temple and its grand plaza.

acts of ritual destruction." They believe that if the intent of those who set the fires was to destroy Teotihuacan politically, then they had to destroy it as a religious center.

After the great city collapsed abruptly in violence and flames, its particular form of communitarian living was never revived in the region. A turbulent time ensued. "The fall of Teotihuacan," wrote the British historian Nigel Davies, "like that of Rome three centuries before, left in its wake a disordered world, whose surviving cities were like planets in orbit round an extinct sun." It was an age of petty kingdoms, of small warring tribal states obsessed with furious conquest. Everything, not least the arts and graces of life, took second place to a preoccupation with security. So desperate was that need that even tribes with different languages banded together into states.

Typical of the thousands of polychrome pottery figurines found in Teotihuacan's ruins, these squat female statuettes wear boldly striped headdresses, shawl-like blouses, and skirts. Traces of color on their raiment suggest that the city's inhabitants customarily wore gaudy hues.

Among those who coalesced from disparate elements were the Toltecs; and it was they who attained predominance over all the rest, becoming the third and last of the Aztecs' great precursors. As with the Olmecs and Teotihuacanos, concrete knowledge of the Toltecs comes almost entirely from archaeology. But here there is a difference: Modern scholars were latecomers, beaten to the Toltecs' treasures by an unruly crowd of brazen amateurs. The Aztecs were early diggers at the Toltecs' capital, Tula. They looted the place with reckless abandon, and when they finished there was not much left to uncover. Determined to ennoble their own shady history and add luster to their people's past, the Aztecs not only claimed to be the inheritors of the Toltecs' mantle but also basked in the reflected glory of their works, plundering whatever they liked for reuse at Tenochtitlan.

The present-day Toltec ruins are, in consequence, unimpressive and hard to reconstruct. Worse yet, the Aztecs' archaeological trophies and their self-serving penchant for historical revision combined to shed more darkness than light on the Toltec past. There was just enough time between the heyday of the Toltecs and the arrival of the Spaniards for the Aztecs to exalt them beyond reality. In Aztec eyes the Toltecs were giants, their capital of Tula a place of great wealth. Even cotton grew in colors, solemnly reported an informant of the Franciscan missionary Bernardino de Sahagún. Not until the 20th century did a picture emerge of Tula as a place precariously perched on the very fringes of central Mexico's arable lands, never far from famine, whose people's arts and crafts were crude and shoddy compared with what had gone before.

Thanks to the Aztecs, everyone had heard of Tula; but none of the early archaeologists knew where to find it. Désiré Charnay, sent back to Mexico by the French government, became convinced on one of his periodic trips that the historic Tula lay underground near a dusty town called Tula de Allende in the state of Hidalgo, one of many Mexican places with that name. He set out to find it.

Digging into some mounds, Charnay struck the black basaltic feet of gigantic statues and fragments of a huge stone rattlesnake, both similar to known Toltec works at Chichen Itza in Yucatan. Clearing away rubbish, he unearthed several apartments of various

Towering stone warriors maintain a stern vigil atop Tula's Pyramid of Quetzalcoatl as the Morning Star (far left, above). Once they served as columns supporting a temple roof.

sizes with frescoed walls, columns, pilasters, benches, and cisterns. Charnay was convinced he had indeed found Tula. But his betters in the world of scholarship looked upon him as a wild romantic and coolly ignored him. Not until the 1930s, when the Mexican anthropologist Wigberto Jiménez Moreno used old place names and geographical landmarks gleaned from historical sources to pinpoint ancient Tula, was the long-dead Charnay proved correct: The Toltec city was exactly where he had said it was.

By the 1970s the systematic work of the American archaeologist Richard Diehl and the Mexican archaeologists Eduardo Matos Moctezuma, Ramón Arellanos Melgarejo, and Lourdes Beauregard de Arellanos had melted the Aztec legends in the crucible of fact. At its zenith from AD 950 to 1150, Tula was a city of at least 30,000 people, far less rigorously planned than Teotihuacan. In its architecture, which "was of majestic conception and mediocre execution," according to the Mexican archaeologist Jorge Acosta, symbols of death and military force predominate. The art is grim, joyless. The base of the most impressive building, a pyramid, is decorated with armed warriors, wild beasts, and eagles eating hearts. The 60-yard-long Serpent Wall depicts snakes devouring human beings whose flesh has been stripped from skulls and bones. There are skull racks and supine figures cradling basins on their abdomens as receptacles for human hearts.

Living quarters in Tula consisted of many small complexes of flat-roofed houses built in groups of three or four around enclosed courtyards, at the center of which were altars or shrines. In their diggings, the archaeologists discovered that Tula's dead were buried in pits under the floors of the houses. Although the routine of daily life at Tula—growing beans and corn, weaving, making ceramics and obsidian goods—appears to have been little different from elsewhere in Mesoamerica, the modern excavations there suggest, in Brian Fagan's words, "a battle-scarred, militaristic civilization, one in which oppression was a way of life and human sacrifice second nature, a far cry from the golden age of Aztec legend."

Tula's end came in a sudden and overwhelming cataclysm. The temples were incinerated, the Serpent Wall toppled, the monuments methodically smashed. Famine and invasion by barbaric peoples from the north are considered to be the likeliest causes, but neither these nor any other single external factor seems sufficient to explain the city's collapse. Perhaps Tula, like Teotihuacan, contained the seeds of its own destruction, encouraging the conditions that sapped its strength. It was a multiethnic city, inhabited by peoples from the north, the Valley of Mexico, and the Gulf Coast, forming a heterogeneous population that spoke several different languages. Richard Diehl, who has dug extensively at Teotihuacan and Tula, has theorized that when economic difficulties eventually arose, "people took sides based on ethnic affiliations," and, as matters worsened, the city lost its ability to absorb the unremitting tide of alien immigrants. And so the gods were smashed, scorned as deities who had forsaken their city. The surviving Toltecs departed and dispersed. By AD 1179 Tula was gone. In time, reoccupied by other peoples, it would rise again into a substantial city esteemed by the Aztecs as the fountain-head of civilization. Then centuries of silence followed.

In words that might speak for Tula, the Aztec philosopher-king Nezalhuacoyotl mused: "All the earth is a grave and nothing escapes it. Nothing is so perfect that it does not descend to its tomb. Rivers, rivulets, and water flow, but never return to their joyful beginnings; anxiously they hasten to the vast realms of the rain god. As they widen their banks, they fashion the sad urn of their burial."

In the political free-for-all in central Mexico that followed the collapse of Tula, not only the remnant Toltecs but the other tribes of Mexico rearranged themselves across the landscape. The most prestigious Toltec lineages gathered in Colhuacan in the southern part of the Valley of Mexico, forming a bastion of culture whose people considered themselves the true heirs of Tula's fallen glory. From the northern deserts, various tribes of barbaric nomads known generally as the Chichimecs—loosely translated as "dog people"—edged southward into the unprotected better lands. Among them and the last to appear were the Aztecs, a semicivilized tribe—"the people whose face nobody knows."

Yet, of course, it was a face all the inhabitants of the Valley of Mexico would soon know. They may not have been interested in the Aztecs, but the Aztecs were interested in them.

THE CITY THAT TIME FORGOT

"The outline of the pyramids is everywhere visible, and serves as a beacon to guide the traveler to the ruins of Teotihuacan," wrote a 19th-century French explorer of this imposing site 25 miles north of Mexico City. Indeed, so awesome is Teotihuacan that pilgrims, archaeologists, and tourists alike have been coming here for more than 1,200 years to ponder its mysteries. Even the Aztecs were wonderstruck. Happening upon the multitiered temples in the 13th century and not knowing who had built them, they gave the haunting place the name Teotihuacan, which in Nahuatl means "city of the gods." It was here, they believed, that the gods had assembled to create the sun and the moon, and it was here that the Aztecs would come regularly as pilgrims to celebrate creation. Cortés and his troops first glimpsed the pyramids in 1520 as they fled from enraged Aztec warriors, but so distraught was the Spanish captain that he failed to tell his king about these towering monuments in his subsequent dispatch. Over the next three centuries, many adventurers and amateur archaeologists arrived in Teotihuacan, searching for gold and speculating on the origin of the crumbling stone structures that dotted the terrain for miles around.

Only during this century have archaeologists cast some light on Teotihuacan's history. By sifting through the ruins, they have discovered that it was much more than a religious complex. Excavations have laid bare a city of unexpected sophistication and proportion—one comparable in scale to imperial Rome—and turned up countless finely crafted artifacts. Playful terra-cotta figurines and ornate masks, such as the funerary piece above carved from onyx, provide valuable information about Teotihuacan society. But the fire-reddened temples and shattered shrines point to a violent end. In AD 500, the city dominated all of Mesoamerica. Two hundred years later it was deserted. All evidence points to a sudden fall, but whether the city was ransacked by its own inhabitants or by invaders remains unknown. As archaeologists continue to dig among its extensive ruins, a host of questions about Teotihuacan and its vanished population await answers.

A man-made mountain 200 feet tall, the Pyramid of the Sun rises from the floor of the Teotihuacan valley. Begun in the first century AD, it took 35 million cubic feet of sun-dried bricks and rubble to finish. Its base, measuring 738 feet on each side, is equal to that of Egypt's Great Pyramid.

This three-foot-diameter stone carving of a skull surrounded by rays was unearthed near the front of the Pyramid of the Sun. It is thought to symbolize the descent of the sun into the world of the dead at the end of the day.

AWESOME ABODE OF THE GODS

During its heyday, when Teotihuacan was a religious mecca for myriad Indian cultures, pilgrims must have been awed by the three-mile-long Avenue of the Dead, a name given the thoroughfare by the Aztecs. Lined with numerous shrines and temples, it lay in the shadow of the city's two major temples, the Pyramid of the Sun and the Pyramid of the Moon, each of which was covered in stucco, ornamented with sculpture, and brightly painted.

The Pyramid of the Sun continues to dominate Teotihuacan in both size and significance. Priests would have had an arduous climb to the top of the 20-story-high structure. From its truncated peak, they could survey the entire city sprawled below as well as gaze heavenward. Trained in astronomy, they kept careful track of the seasons and presided over the continuous cycles of public ritual. The religious importance of the Pyramid of the Sun is supported by the 1971 discovery of a lava cave below it containing offerings. Archaeologists suspect that the pyramid was built over the cave after it had become a shrine and goal for pilgrims.

MAPPING THE REMAINS OF A METROPOLIS

In the 1960s, a French-born American archaeologist named René Millon, convinced that Teotihuacan had been not just a religious center but a city of unimagined size and complexity, embarked on an ambitious mapping project to prove his point. He would define the boundaries of the ancient city and record its every archaeological and topographical feature.

Millon first had the city photographed from the air so that a topographical map could be prepared. Then he and a team of experts trudged over a 10-square-mile area, collecting shards and filling out record sheets for each structure they encountered. Five years later the project was complete, and the results were staggering: More than 2,200 apartment complexes had been identified. The evidence was incontrovertible—Teotihuacan had at one time been a flourishing metropolis with a population possibly as great as 200,000.

This schematic map shows a 5.5-square-mile area of Teotihuacan that includes the Avenue of the Dead, lined with shrines and palaces and surrounded by apartment compounds (small black rectangles). *The much-larger map developed by the archaeologists encompasses the entire city and notes every surviving structure within the quadrants into which the city was divided.*

1 Avenue of the Dead
2 Citadel
3 Feathered Serpent Temple
4 Great Compound
5 Sun Pyramid
6 Quetzalpapalotl Palace
7 Moon Pyramid

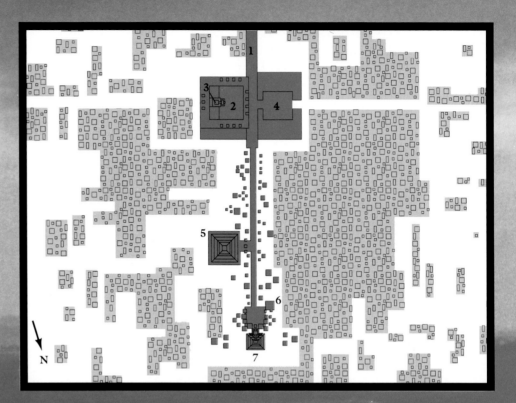

HOUSING OF A HIGHER ORDER

The architecture of the apartment compound below, only one of many such one-story dwellings in the city, must have afforded the residents a great deal of privacy. The windowless exterior buffered noise from the street and helped keep the interior cool by day and warm by night. Rooms surrounded a spacious patio that let in light and air and had drains to carry away rainwater. Typically, a large platform off the patio served as a small temple.

Many of the occupants farmed land outside the city, but others worked as artisans, exchanging their goods in a central marketplace. Teotihuacan was the center of a thriving obsidian trade, and many workshops were devoted to chipping the volcanic glass into tools and weapons. Others specialized in pottery, stone, gems, cloth, leather, and wood- and featherwork. In the teeming marketplace, people from the entire region intermingled. Native inhabitants lived in barrios, or neighborhoods, which contained a rich mixture of classes and professions; but in at least one area of the city, foreigners occupied their own sharply defined quarter.

A portion of a mural reconstruction from an apartment compound in the northeastern part of the city shows common people frolicking in water and on land. Scholars think that the mural may illustrate an origin myth.

A terra-cotta figurine of a woman at her ease is one of thousands of pieces produced by Teotihuacan craftsmen—often using molds—that depict ordinary mortals as well as deities. This one is only four and a half inches high.

This brazier lid, believed to represent Quetzalpapalotl, the quetzal-butterfly god, is decorated top and bottom with attributes of the deity. The plume protruding from the headdress is a stylized butterfly proboscis.

AT HOME WITH THE NOBILITY

The elite lived well in Teotihuacan. Their palatial homes were scattered throughout the city. Many lay not far from the two grand boulevards that divided Teotihuacan into four parts, the Avenue of the Dead and the so-called East-West Avenue, while those of priests and nobles occupied ground near the great pyramids, well insulated from the hubbub that prevailed where the streets were narrowest. Today their collapsed walls and faded murals belie their former grandeur.

The Quetzalpapalotl Palace *(below)*, located just southwest of the Pyramid of the Moon, is one of the most extensively studied residences. Here, in 1962, archaeologists uncovered a central patio surrounded by richly decorated rooms embellished with colorful frescoes. Stone columns, bearing elaborate bas-reliefs of quetzal-butterflies and water symbols, hold up the roof of the arcade around the patio to which the inhabitants could retreat for shade during the brightest part of the day.

THE CENTER OF GREATNESS

Teotihuacan's two axial streets intersect at the enclosure called the Citadel *(lower left)*. This complex, with its 11-acre square plaza, could have served as an assembly point where throngs gathered to witness ceremonies.

Given the immensity of the site and the presence of the ruins of two palaces and a highly ornate temple, archaeologists suspect that the Citadel was the political center of Teotihuacan. Yet information on the city's ruling class remains elusive. Frustrated by the paucity of evidence, archaeologists have recently concentrated on the Citadel's seven-tiered Feathered Serpent Temple *(near center of Citadel at lower left)* for clues. Ornamented with rows of alternating stone serpents, shells, and goggle-eyed faces, it is by far the city's most elaborate religious monument. If heads of state were buried within Teotihuacan, archaeologists reason, the temple would have been their most likely resting place.

Stone serpent heads like this one, wreathed with feathers, decorate the western facade of the magnificent Feathered Serpent Temple. Traces of the original red mineral paint can still be seen on the feathers.

GRIMNESS AT THE TEMPLE'S HEART

Hoping to fathom the secrets of the Feathered Serpent Temple, a team of Mexican archaeologists set out to excavate along its southern edge in 1983. Days later they were rewarded with a spectacular find. Deep in the volcanic soil they came upon three burial pits. The largest, some 26 feet long, contained 18 skeletons. With their arms tucked behind their vertebrae and their wrists crossed as if tied, there was little question that these individuals had been sacrificed.

Then, in 1988, a joint team of Mexican and American archaeologists started digging toward the center of the temple. Eighty feet in, they came upon a tunnel made by tomb robbers and the sparse remains of two heavily looted burials. Fortunately, the thieves had missed the central burial. The excited diggers painstakingly unearthed 20 skeletons, all sacrificial victims, who had been interred with rich offerings. Despite the significance of the find, the archaeologists were disappointed by the absence of a royal burial. Whether such a burial exists, or whether, if it exists, it was looted long ago, only further excavations can tell.

These two skeletons were among a group found in 1988 on the east side of the temple. The one to the left wears a collar from which nine human upper jaws are suspended. Above this necklace can be seen a choker made of imitation teeth carved from shell.

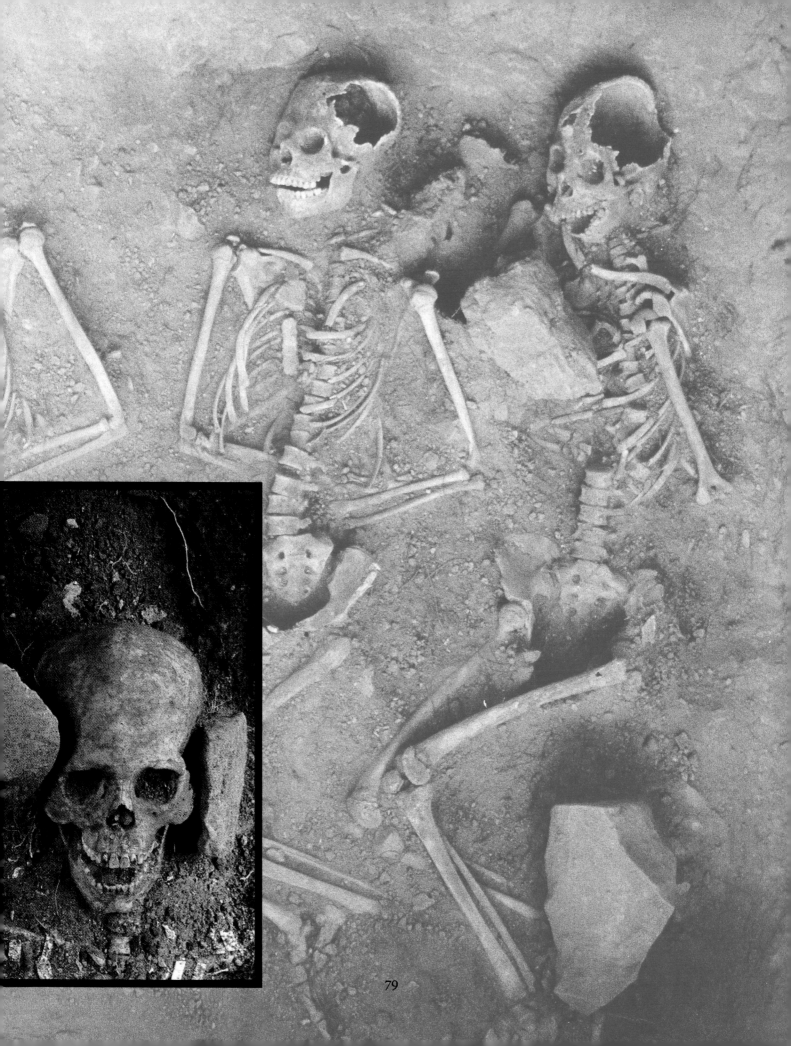

THE TERRIBLE SUSTENANCE OF THE GODS

A smiling skull, embellished with eyes of iron pyrite and bits of turquoise and jet, may have belonged to a youth who for a year personified Tezcatlipoca, omnipotent god of the Aztecs. When his time was up, he was ritually sacrificed.

February 21, 1978, would be a day to remember. Workmen digging ditches for new electric cable in the heart of Mexico City had penetrated the street's concrete pavement and dug down six feet when their shovels struck a large, flat, round stone. Scraping away some of the dirt covering it, they could see a carved surface. This, they knew, was a discovery that the Archaeological Recovery Office would want to know about, and a call was made to the authorities. When a team of excited archaeologists arrived, its members removed more of the dirt to reveal a horrific scene cut into the stone—the severed head, arms, legs, and torso of a woman strewn in a circle almost 11 feet in diameter. Except for jewelry and a serpent belt adorned with a human skull, she was naked. Studying the stone, the archaeologists identified the figure as the moon goddess Coyolxauhqui, sister of Huitzilopochtli, the warrior sun god and Aztec patron deity.

Under any circumstances this would have been considered a major find, but what made it all the more significant was that it occurred at the spot where *el Templo Mayor,* the Great Temple, principal shrine of the Aztec capital of Tenochtitlan, had stood. Indeed, the discovery would launch one of the century's most fascinating archaeological excavations *(pages 108-123),* in which large portions of the Great Temple would emerge into daylight after being buried for centuries in the spongy soil of Mexico City. By extension, the stone would serve to illuminate the importance of war and human sacrifice to the functioning of the Aztec state, for Coyolxauhqui played a crucial role in one of the central Aztec myths.

This myth told of a time in the distant past when Huitzilopochtli wreaked vengeance on his sister, Coyolxauhqui. The story goes that Coatlicue, their mother, after having given birth to the moon and 400 stars, had taken a vow of chastity. But one day, as she was sweeping out the shrine atop the sacred mountain where she lived, she was impregnated by a ball of feathers. Her offspring were outraged when they heard of their mother's pregnancy, convinced that she had broken her vow. Coyolxauhqui rallied them, and together they agreed to kill Coatlicue for her transgression. But one child ran to inform the still-unborn Huitzilopochtli of their plans. When the band approached to do their murderous work, the infant sun god sprang forth fully armed from his mother's womb and cut the vengeful moon goddess Coyolxauhqui down before chasing after his other siblings—a mythical expression of the rising sun's daily defeat of the moon and the stars. In his anger, he hacked Coyolxauhqui to pieces and threw all but her head down the mountainside.

The newly found stone did more than echo this ancient myth. Its placement at the bottom of the stairs leading to the top of the Great Temple recalled Coyolxauhqui's fate, for it had served a gruesome purpose, which was to catch the bodies of sacrificial victims hurled from the killing stone in front of Huitzilopochtli's shrine, one of two shrines that adorned the flat summit. Bouncing and skidding down the bloody steps of the man-made mountain, the bodies landed on the Coyolxauhqui stone in the chaotic poses of death.

Driven by fear of the gods, particularly Huitzilopochtli, the Aztecs performed human sacrifice on a scale unknown either before or since in history. The conquistador Bernal Díaz del Castillo was an eyewitness to this bloodletting and wrote vividly of the fate of some of his friends, whom the Aztecs had captured during the climactic

Still lying where it was found in 1978 at the foot of the Great Temple in Mexico City, the stone bearing a relief of the dismembered body of the goddess Coyolxauhqui is protected by temporary metal scaffolding. It was subsequently moved to the Museum of the Great Temple and today is regarded as one of Mexico's greatest archaeological treasures.

battle between the Indians and the Spaniards for control of the city in the spring of 1521. From the place to which Díaz had been forced to retreat, he could see the temple. At the terrifying sound of the Huitzilopochtli shrine drum, which was accompanied by the blare of conchs, horns, and trumpetlike instruments, Díaz glanced toward the Great Temple and saw that some of his comrades, who had been captured by the Aztecs, were being dragged to the top to be sacrificed. When the Indians had gotten them "to a small square where their accursed idols are kept," recounted Díaz in the breathless style of someone who has beheld horror and never been able to forget it, "we saw them place plumes on the head of many of our men and with things like fans in their hands they forced them to dance before Huitzilopochtli, and after they had danced they placed them on their backs on some rather narrow stones which had been prepared as places for sacrifice, and with stone knives they sawed open their chests and drew out their palpitating hearts and offered them to the idols that were there, and they kicked the bodies down the steps, and Indian butchers who were waiting below cut off the arms and feet and flayed the skin off the faces, and prepared it afterward like glove leather with the beards on, and kept those for the festivals when they celebrated drunken orgies, and the flesh they ate with chilies."

The butchery that was so incomprehensible to Díaz and his fellow Spaniards would, of course, have recalled to those who carried it out the ritual dismemberment of the goddess and the triumph of the fierce and vengeful Huitzilopochtli, deity not just of the sun but of war and warriors—the presiding genius of the Aztec people.

If ever there was a people dedicated to martial prowess, it was the warring Aztecs. Nothing was more honorable in their eyes than a manly death in combat, or as a captive offered up to the gods on the sacrificial stone. Warriors who died in battle or as human sacrifices and women who perished in childbirth were deemed worthy of an afterlife; almost all others, regardless of status and rank, wandered for four years through the underworld until they reached its lowest level, which the Aztecs called the Land of the Dead, or "our common home," presented their gifts to the Lord of Death, and then disappeared into the shadows. Aztec orators praised, in particular, the glorious end of men on the battlefield. Indeed, the records tell of one thanking his creator for allowing him "to see these many deaths of my brothers and nephews." Their poets sang of such a passing. One

Superimposed over excavations of the Great Temple, this outline of the pyramid suggests its appearance when Cortés arrived at Tenochtitlan in 1519. The shrine on the right honored the rain god, Tlaloc, the one on the left Huitzilopochtli, the Aztecs' patron deity.

wrote: "There is nothing like death in war, nothing like the flowery death so precious to him who gives life. Far off I see it: My heart yearns for it!" Another spoke lyrically of the battlefield: "Where the burning, divine liquor is poured out, where the divine eagles are blackened with smoke, where the jaguars roar, where gems and rich jewels are scattered, where feathers wave like spume, there, where the warriors tear each other and noble princes are smashed to pieces."

The Aztecs even viewed birth as a battleground, full of pain and blood. When a baby boy came into the world, the midwife held onto him, as though he were her captive, and let out war cries. She then exhorted the child to heed her words. "Thy home is not here," she intoned, "for thou art an eagle or a jaguar"—a lone predator. "Here is only the place of thy nest," she told the infant. "War is thy task. Thou shalt give drink, nourishment, food to the sun." She was referring, of course, to blood. The battlefield was viewed as a sacred place, and the midwife went on to speak of the honor of dying on it as a warrior or as a captive on the sacrificial stone: "Perhaps thou wilt merit death by the obsidian knife." Poets elaborated on the nobility of such a death. "May his heart not falter," goes one incantation to a god on behalf of a warrior. "May he desire, may he long for the flowery death by the obsidian knife. May he savor the scent, savor the freshness, savor the sweetness of the darkness." Little boys destined to be warriors were presented with miniature shields and arrows symbolizing the goal of their future existence; their umbilical cords and the weapons they had been given were entrusted to warriors for ceremonial burial on a battlefield.

Part of the reason for this military emphasis was religious. The sun's struggle with the moon and the stars had to be resumed each night, and if Huitzilopochtli were to lose the battle, life would come to an end in a shroud of darkness. His strength had to be constantly replenished, and to Aztec eyes the surest nourishment lay in human blood, which they referred to as "most precious water." So there was a constant demand for sacrificial victims. Scholars vary in their tallies of the number of people the Aztecs killed every year, but perhaps as many as 20,000 were sacrificed throughout the empire.

There were other reasons for the cultivation of warfare. Like its exact historical contemporary, Renaissance Italy, Mexico in the time of the Aztecs was a land of city-states. Dozens of small urban centers, each one controlling an area of surrounding land large enough to feed its own population, vied for power. The one that could strike terror in the hearts of all the others would dominate and rule—and exact the greatest tribute. Another condition that fostered warfare, curiously enough, was the unusual agricultural fertility of the Valley of Mexico, whose nutritional riches had been further boosted through the use of *chinampas,* small garden plots anchored in lakes, spread with woven twigs on which was piled fertile muck brought up from the bottom. The result was that comparatively little labor was needed to produce enough food to live on. One modern estimate suggests that a family could have supported itself through the year on the fruits of only about seven weeks' work. Part of the resulting crop surplus went to feed the cities in the form of tribute; but a labor surplus remained, leaving men able to pursue militaristic ambitions. One effect was to produce a hierarchical social structure, in which different groups of people emerged, such as warrior and priestly classes.

In a world of conflicting states, there was much to be gained, as the Aztecs were to find out, by refining the art of warfare. Aztec codices, Spanish accounts of the conquest, and archaeological evidence show that military technology in Mesoamerica did not run to elaborate siege engines or other complex machinery of war. Success or failure on the battlefield depended instead on the efficient training of individual warriors. Under the circumstances, the victorious nation was likely to be the one that excelled in two fields: the organization of its fighting force and the morale of its warriors. The Aztecs' entire culture was effectively structured to maximize both of these.

The process began at the highest level. The Aztec throne did not automatically pass to the eldest son; instead an element of selection was involved. A council of warriors, priests, and various officials chose the future monarch from within the ranks of the royal family; military leadership and priestly aptitude were perhaps the most important of the criteria involved in the choice.

Soon after ascending the throne, the new ruler was expected to lead his troops on a campaign of conquest. The success of this initial expedition was a vital test of his mettle. When one new ruler, Tizoc, came back with only 40 captives after losing 300 men, he was branded a failure and his reputation never recovered. His reign lasted only five years. Ac-

APPEASING AN APPETITE FOR HEARTS AND BLOOD

The Aztecs believed that in creating the world, their gods gave their hearts and blood to the sun, and that as the gods' beneficiaries, they must make a similar sacrifice to keep the universe in perfect balance. Although most of their deities required regular sacrifice, the one who needed the most nourishment was their patron, the war god Huitzilopochtli. It was thought that without his daily fortifica-

tion of human hearts and blood, he would lack the strength to do battle with the forces of night—and would fail to rise as the sun the next morning.

The codex illustration at left depicts the standard rite at the Great Temple at Tenochtitlan, with a priest cutting out the heart of a captive, whose blood spills down the stairs. The heart rises heavenward here; in reality it would have been deposited cording to one chronicler, "Members of his court, angered by his weakness and lack of desire to bring glory to the Aztec nation, helped him to die with something they gave him to eat."

In view of his dismal military reputation, it is ironic that this ruler is now best remembered as the dedicatee of the triumphal Stone of Tizoc, a massive circular monument eight and a half feet across by three feet high that is today a treasure of the National Museum of Anthropology in Mexico City. Although carvings depicting Aztec triumphs decorate the rim, only one can be linked to Tizoc's known campaigns, and scholars now think that the reliefs celebrate the empire he inherited rather than just his own sparse victories. (A similar stone, apparently depicting the exploits of a far more successful monarch, Motecuhzoma I, was unearthed from the garden of the Archbishop's Palace in Mexico City in 1988.)

Behind the Aztec emphasis on martial triumph lay a compelling logic. Interestingly, the Aztecs made little attempt to subjugate the peoples they conquered. No chain of fortresses kept the defeated nations under the yoke; even permanent military garrisons seem to have been rare. Instead, the conquerors depended on intimidation for the continued submission of the other city-states of the region: The fear of retaliatory action was what kept the tribute flowing. Any hint that Aztec armies were no longer invincible could therefore spark defiance and insurrection—a fact the Spanish conquistadors were to capitalize on when hostile Indian groups allied with them to help accomplish the Aztecs' overthrow.

Until that final, unforeseeable cataclysm, however, the Aztec war machine was about as effective a weapon as, in the existing state of technology, it could have been. All the energies of the state were directed to encouraging martial prowess. From the age of 20, every able-bodied male was liable to be drafted for the campaigns that were a regular part of the Aztec year, usually starting in the late autumn, after the harvest had been completed and the summer rains had come to an end. In addition, there was also a professional military class, drawn from both the nobility and the commoners who

in a special receptacle, such as the immense stone jaguar pictured above.

But the heart was not the only organ to receive ritual treatment. Xipe Totec, a god associated with springtime, demanded human sacrifice in an annual rite of renewal. After prisoners perished during a mock battle ceremony, their bodies were flayed, and penitents wore the skins for 20 days. The figure at right shows Xipe Totec in the gruesome garb.

had proved their valor in war. These full-time fighters had no other commitments but warfare, as they were supported by the state largely from the supply of tribute provided by conquered cities.

All boys received some military training. At the age of about 10, their hair was shorn but for a lock on the nape of the neck as a preliminary initiation into the sacred ranks of the warrior. When they turned 15 they received weapons training, meeting every evening with veterans who regaled them with tales of war and taught them the requisite dances and chants. They were also given tasks designed to toughen them, such as carrying logs from far-distant forests to the temples, where these were fed to the eternal fires kept burning there.

Each boy had to retain his telltale tuft of hair until he had participated in the capture of a prisoner. His first experience on the battlefield was limited to carrying a warrior's shield and observing the action, but his second required that he participate, with as many as five of his fellow novices, in taking alive a foe. The captive was then taken to those men in charge of sacrifice, who killed him. The body was divided up among the boys for their ritualistic consumption: The right thigh and torso went to the youngster who had behaved most heroically; the left thigh went to the second bravest youth; the right upper arm to the third—and so on until no part was left.

Having proved himself, the new warrior had his lock cut off and let his hair grow to cover his right ear. But now he was on his own. No longer could he count on the assistance of his friends, nor could he give any help to them in their next battle, even when he saw that a companion was in trouble—if he were to go to his aid, he ran the risk of being accused of trying to steal the other's potential captive. And he was strictly enjoined not to take pity on a friend who had failed to capture a prisoner during a battle; giving him one of his own would be cheating punishable by death.

The goal of such conflict was to try to engage

The Stone of Tizoc, carved during that unsuccessful ruler's five-year reign and measuring eight and a half feet in diameter, illustrates a series of military campaigns, in only one of which Tizoc himself participated. At the center of the sun-disk top is a depression that may have held hearts from human sacrifices.

a foe whose status equaled or exceeded the fighter's own and to subdue him without inflicting too much injury. Mutilated prisoners did not make fit subjects for sacrifice. For each man he took alive, the aspiring warrior received special mantles, and thus his military record became visible for all to see at any time. Those young men who failed to distinguish themselves on the battlefield by seizing captives risked being subjected to ridicule and reduced to living a humble life.

The principle of public recompense was further extended once a warrior had four or more captives to his name. He then became an honored soldier with the right to his share of the tribute from vassal states and might even qualify for a seat on the war council, which advised the ruler on military matters. In addition, the warrior was eligible to assume senior responsibilities in civil life, such as administering the schools where the children of commoners were trained. Elaborate laws decreed the exact dress and regalia to which his military exploits entitled him. Indeed, under the advice of Tlacaelel, a general who served as a kind of grand vizier to three 15th-century monarchs, such a hero became the recipient of only the finest jewels and the best cloaks and shields. To preserve the exclusivity of these awards, no one could buy them in the marketplace.

In further recognition of his accomplishments, the seasoned warrior, especially if he were a nobleman, might be summoned to join one of the elite societies of professional fighting men that helped make the Aztec armies so formidable in the field. The aristocratic Order of the Eagle and the Jaguar Knights had supreme standing. The titles the knights bore were proud ones, calling to mind the supreme air and land predators of the Mesoamerican natural world. The Aztecs considered the eagle "fearless," a "brave, daring" bird, a "wing beater, a screamer" that could "gaze into, face, the sun," qualities to emulate. They saw the jaguar as "cautious, wise, proud," a powerful animal that deflected a hunter's arrows before stirring, stretching, and then springing upon its attacker.

Young nobles who had distinguished themselves on the battlefield received enhanced military training, particularly in the use of the Aztec wooden, obsidian-edged sword, a weapon that functioned primarily as a club. Their privileges included the right to keep concubines and to dine in the royal palace. Moreover, each order had its own house in the palace, where the war council met to discuss military matters in the presence of the ruler. The so-called Hall of the Eagle Knights—discovered as the temple was being excavated—

AZTEC WARRIORS: THE TRAPPINGS AND PARAPHERNALIA OF POWER

One way to assure the Aztecs' bloodthirsty gods a steady stream of living sacrifices was to capture them on the battlefield. Warriors who brought them home were showered with gifts and honors, among which were the fine capes and headdresses seen here in illustrations from various codices. Such raiment was intended not merely to adorn the warrior but also to proclaim his rank—which was determined primarily by the number of men seized in battle.

When a soldier took his first captive, the ruler awarded him a cloak decorated with a scorpion or a flower design, along with various other garments. The fighter who took his second prisoner received a mantle trimmed in red. And in recognition of his having taken a third captive, he was entitled to wear a lavishly worked cloak called an *ehehcailacatzcozcatl*—meaning "wind-twisted jewel." With four captives to his credit, he advanced into the upper echelon of the military classes and could wear his hair in their distinctive style. He also received new weapons, special insignia, and additional garments and ceremonial gear.

When he became recognized as a *tequihuah,* or veteran warrior, he could join the ranks of the elite Eagle and Jaguar Knights *(overleaf)* and wear their distinctive uniforms. In time, he might rise to the rank of general or serve as an adviser in the ruler's councils. But in climbing the ranks, he also put himself at increasing risk: The accouterments of success made him a conspicuous target on the battlefield.

Depending on the number of enemy soldiers they captured, the warriors shown here with their captives could dress in ever more resplendent finery.

In battle, warriors shed their awkward robes in favor of tighter-fitting garb but kept the headdresses and insignia that announced their status.

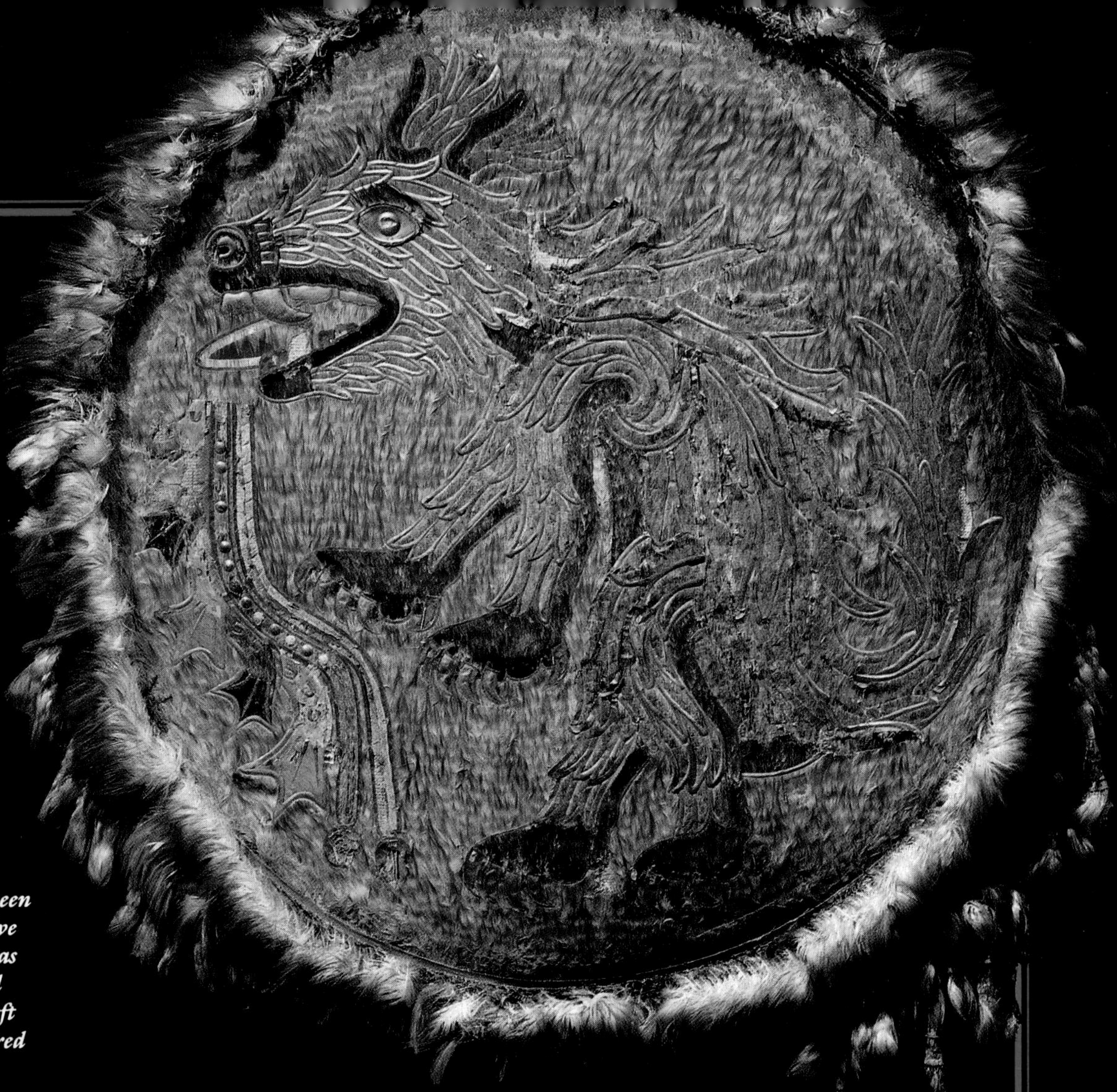

This feathered ceremonial shield, sporting a fierce coyote, would have been awarded to a warrior who performed well in battle.

Exceptional warriors, seen below, earned distinctive office or rank, which was marked by their special dress. The one at far left was known as an honored cuauhnochtecuhtli, *or* eagle prickly-pear lord.

SERVANTS OF THE SUN GOD — THE EAGLES AND THE JAGUARS

Upon deliverance of his fourth captive for sacrifice, the seasoned warrior entered the knighthood and as either an Eagle or a Jaguar Knight came to serve the god of the sun, Tonatiuh. These two elite societies—with no apparent conceptual differences between them—admitted both nobles and commoners. The nobles, whose titles were hereditary, far outnumbered the others, however, because they were given better opportunities to distinguish themselves in battle.

After initiation into the corps, Eagles and Jaguars enjoyed many privileges. As in the case of other warriors of high standing, they were exempt from taxation and tribute. In addition, they could keep concubines, eat human flesh, drink *octli,* which was alcoholic, in public, and dine in the royal palace. The rare warrior who rose to knighthood from humble origins received land as well; and his children could inherit his noble status, although such a family was denied other privileges available to blue bloods.

Gathering at the *cuauhcalli,* their quarters in the palace at Tenochtitlan, Eagles and Jaguars hosted war councils with the ruler and his officers. There they also convened for worship of Tonatiuh and for business, as well as for pleasure—in the form of cannibalistic feasts.

Shown actual size, this flint knife, with mosaic handle in the shape of an Eagle warrior, was probably used in sun-god worship ceremonies.

In the inner sanctum at the Temple of Malinalco, outside the capital, new Eagle and Jaguar warriors probably underwent the sacred initiation rites of their orders. Here a low platform curves around an eagle effigy.

A codex drawing illustrates the battle regalia of the Knights of the Sun—an Eagle warrior dressed in an eagle-headed helmet and feathers (left) and a Jaguar wearing the animal's skin.

comprises an entrance hall connected by a corridor to a courtyard with two adjoining chambers. The rooms are furnished with benches decorated with carved reliefs of soldiers and serpents. In one of the inner chambers, twin processions converge on the carved image of a *zacatapayolli*—a ball of plaited grass into which bloodied spines from the maguey plant, traditionally used for self-laceration, have been inserted as an offering. Two enigmatic ceramic skeletal figures were found flanking the entrance to one of the chambers.

Arrayed for battle, these elite warriors wore eagle or jaguar costumes. Archaeologists have unearthed sculptures that suggest the fearsome appearance the Eagle and Jaguar Knights must have presented. A 30-inch-high stone statue now in Mexico City's National Museum of Anthropology shows a squatting figure, his head emerging from a jaguar's gaping maw. Even more extraordinary are two life-size images of Eagle Knights, executed in fired clay, discovered on either side of another entryway to the rooms of the order. The warriors' faces peer out from open beaks; their arms are encased in feathered sleeves that flare out like wings, almost as though the men were about to take off. The presence of the Eagle Knight figures in the temple has led scholars to assume that the complex was used for some of the order's ceremonies. Given the proximity of the Great Temple to the royal palace, it is likely that the ruler himself might have come here to sit in council with his leading warriors.

Among the other prestigious orders were the *otontin*—named after a tribe admired for its fierceness—and the *cuahchicqueh,* or "shorn ones." The cuahchicqueh sported a single lock of hair over one ear braided with red ribbon and painted their bare pates red and blue. The otontin also wore a lock, but they tied theirs close to their otherwise shaven heads so that it would wave above them in battle. Members rose through the ranks in reward for their combative skill. The cuahchicqueh in particular were noted for their valor; they fought in pairs and were sworn not to take a single step backward on the battlefield or ever to retreat, despite the odds. If one fell dead or wounded, the other had to fight on alone. They formed the shock troops that won many famous victories.

Behind them the common soldiers were organized in bands of 20 that were in turn grouped into larger companies of either 200 or 400 men. Each urban district of Tenochtitlan provided a number of such companies, each one commanded by an officer chosen from the ranks of those who had taken four or more captives. The companies were themselves arranged in regiments linked to the four quarters of the capital. The forces from Tenochtitlan were bolstered by additional troops provided by two other city-states in response to a triple alliance that their rulers had set up for economic and military reasons. Mercenaries were also sometimes used, among them aggressive northern hunters who served as bowmen.

The Aztec army was a splendid and terrifying sight as it prepared for battle. In keeping with the ceremonial nature of Mesoamerican warfare, the troops dressed for display as well as for effective fighting. Although little in the way of Aztec arms and armor has survived, the codices and Spanish sources have good descriptions of the panoply of war. The basic protective garment, available mostly to proven warriors and members of the military orders, was an armor of quilted, brine-saturated cotton, about two fingers thick. It proved so effective against arrows that the Spanish conquistadors learned to prefer it to their own chain mail. Over this the soldiers wore feathered tunics decorated with skirtlike hanging borders of feathers, or else body-encasing jumpsuits of heavy cloth. These were also often covered in multicolored feathers, sometimes cleverly sewn to resemble animal pelts or the features of gods or demons. Nobles and leading warriors occasionally wore helmets that mimicked the heads of beasts of prey. Virtually all combatants carried round shields, usually made of cane or flame-hardened wood reinforced with leather and faced with feather ornamentation.

In addition, officers carried standards strapped tightly to their backs by means of shoulder harnesses. Besides advertising the rank of their wearer, these towering basketwork emblems, often splendidly decorated with featherwork, gems, silver, or gold, served a vital communications function. In the din of battle they enabled commanders to locate individual companies and also served as rallying points for the soldiers within each unit. Their very visibility was to make the standard-bearers tempting targets for the Spaniards; not the least of the reasons for the conquistadors' supremacy in battle against the Aztecs was to be the relative ease with which they could dismantle the enemy's system of communications.

The offensive weapons the warriors carried included bows up to five feet long, firing arrows tipped with sharpened flint or chipped obsidian. They wielded slings made from the fiber of the maguey that hurled specially shaped stones 300 yards or more and could stun a man, if not kill him. Wooden darts, their tips fire-hardened, were flung from *atlatls*, hooked spear-throwers whose use increased the force of the projectile by more than 50 percent. Lances longer than the soldiers who used them were edged with blades of obsidian sharp enough to shave with. There were clubs with heads of wood or stone. Most formidable of all, however, were the clubs made of wood but armed with glass-sharp obsidian chips inserted into grooves along their cutting edges and fixed in place with turtle-dung glue. Some were designed for two-handed use; the Spaniards said of them that they could strike the head off a horse at a single blow.

This richly carved and gilded spear-thrower, known as an atlatl, probably served a ceremonial, rather than functional, purpose. In warfare, atlatls enabled warriors to hurl darts with enough force to pierce some types of armor.

Not all of these weapons had equal status. Bows were associated with the hunting tribes to the north, barbarians in Aztec eyes, and so they were the arms of the lower orders. By way of contrast, the nobility, trained from their youth in the use of heavy weapons, wielded the great clubs and halberdlike spears that proved so formidable in hand-to-hand combat. As a result, they probably suffered fewer battlefield casualties than the commoners and took more prisoners, thereby reinforcing their position at the top of the social tree.

The battles these warriors fought were for the most part ferocious and confused melees in which there was plenty of room for individuals to make their mark. In their heroism and intensity they must have resembled the conflicts of Homer's Greece more than the armored clashes of the Europe of their day. Typically, combat would begin with a fusillade of arrows and stones. The troops, stretched out in a long line, would then close, hurling javelins from their atlatls as they approached the enemy lines. With the hardened veterans of the military orders in the Aztec vanguard, the front lines of the opposing armies would clash, and hand-to-hand fighting would ensue. These tactics encouraged frontal fighting and explain the popularity of long thrusting weapons.

One of the oddest features of the battles to the

An ornate helmet, worn probably by an aristocrat in ritual ceremonies, preserves only portions of the turquoise, mother-of-pearl, malachite, and pink shell mosaic that once covered it entirely.

eyes of Europeans was that little emphasis was put on annihilating the enemy. Killing a man on the battlefield served no purpose, for a wounded or maimed captive would be unfit for temple sacrifice. Rather than use the sharp side of his club on the victim, the warrior would probably have struck him with its flat side to stun him. More likely, he would have tried to weaken and exhaust his adversary so that he would falter and faint, as related in the Florentine Codex, and throw "himself down as if dead, as if he wished that breath might end." Thus could the foe be seized intact for subsequent sacrifice.

Tactics were not unknown to Mesoamerican armies. The importance of flanking was appreciated, and here the length of the Aztec line—for, as the imperial masters, they normally managed to field more men than their opponents—proved more than helpful. In addition, the Aztecs successfully employed the age-old stratagem of the feigned retreat. One account describes how soldiers of the otontin and cuahchicqueh orders were instructed before a battle to prepare an ambush. "All these soldiers were ordered to lie down upon the earth with their shields and clubs in their hands, about 2,000 men from all the provinces. They were then covered with grass until not a man could be seen." When the opposing army appeared, the Aztecs remained still. "They ran to the place where the great warriors waited in ambush. When the enemy had entered the trap, the men concealed by the grass stood up and annihilated them. Not one escaped; all were killed or taken prisoner. Even the youths took many captives."

After a victory—and the Aztecs lost few battles in the course of building their empire—the winners rarely sought to destroy the opposition. The losing city-state would be offered terms. If its leaders proved obdurate, the victors might enter their city and fire the main temple: A glyph depicting a burning temple was the Aztec symbol for victory. Such an act was a devastating blow to a city's pride; it implied that the local god had been overcome. But it also had vital practical significance. The temple was usually a town's most heavily fortified site and also the seat of the principal armory, so its destruction meant the end of effective resistance. Even so, the conquering troops rarely went on to devastate the civilian districts—a policy that would not

97

have served Aztec interests, as it would have reduced the amount of tribute the losers could pay. Similarly, the conquerors were normally content to leave the existing royal house in place, so long as its leader agreed to fulfill his people's obligations to the victor.

The goal of military action was to force defeated nations to accept Aztec hegemony and to pay tribute. By 1519, some 370 towns had come to such an arrangement, and the amount of goods that arrived annually in Tenochtitlan was staggering. It included an estimated 7,000 tons of corn, 4,000 tons of beans, and two million cotton cloaks, along with smaller numbers of war costumes, shields, and feather headdresses. The arrival of such tribute was a wonder to behold, reported the Spanish chronicler Durán. In addition to basic commodities, there might be live birds, including green, red, and blue parrots, snarling jaguars and wildcats, "great and small snakes, some poisonous, others not, some fierce, others harmless; toasted locusts, winged ants, large cicadas and little ones," and a wide range of gourds, "some carved, some gilded and painted," with one flat type used "in the same way that we use silver trays or large plates to carry the food to the table or to give water for the hands."

Of the luxury products unobtainable in the Valley of Mexico, many that came as tribute to the Aztec capital have been unearthed in the course of the excavation of the Great Temple and are now on display in the on-site museum. Among them are greenstone carvings from the southern region of Guerrero, vast quantities of shells and coral from the coastal states, obsidian from the state of Hidalgo, and alabaster goods from the state of Puebla, in central Mexico.

The Aztec system of enforcing voluntary submission on the neighboring fiefdoms has left fewer monuments for archaeologists to investigate than if chains of fortresses had marked the triumphant passage of the nation's armies. One recovered site, however, still retains something of the brooding splendor of the empire's latter days. The ruins of Malinalco stand on a hillside about 70 miles southwest of Mexico City, in a region that had only recently been conquered when the Aztecs decided to build there at the turn of the 16th century. The complex they constructed seems to have served both as a ritual and an administrative center, and the exact reasons the Aztecs chose to erect it are unclear. But Malinalco lay close to the border of their empire, with the undefeated and hostile land of Michoacan not far beyond. Whatever its exact function, the place was in part a frontier outpost.

An air of mystery surrounds the complex's best-preserved building, a small, circular temple whose entrance is in the form of a gaping serpent's mouth. In the center of the cool, dark interior, a carved stone eagle, its wings outstretched, faces the doorway. A stone bench running around the back of the chamber is decorated with an eagle-and-jaguar motif. In the center a jaguar skin is carved, its head and paws rising from the seat rim.

The building was probably intended to commemorate Aztec military prowess, but there may also have been a deeper symbolism at work. The Malinalco area was associated in Mexican minds with the goddess Malinalxochitl, a sinister deity sometimes confused with the rebellious Coyolxauhqui. Like Coyolxauhqui, Malinalxochitl was a disruptive force, an evil sorceress who, in the days of the Aztecs' early wanderings, supposedly commanded a faction of the people. On Huitzilopochtli's orders, the rest of the people abandoned her and her followers overnight, whereupon she founded the town of Malinalco. The 16th-century chronicler who related the story went on to comment that "the people of Malinalco to this day have the reputation of being sorcerers, and it is said that they inherited this gift from the woman who founded the city."

The gods of the Malinalco area were earth deities believed to live in caves. Perhaps that is why, in such a dangerous and supernatural frontier region, the Aztecs apparently chose to symbolize their final victory over the dissident followers of Malinalxochitl by carving a cave of their own and filling it with all the symbolism of the empire's military might. As the jaguar seat was the special preserve of the Aztec ruler, it may even be that occasionally he came in person to sit in council in the dark temple, symbolically watching over the conquered lands from his eagle's aerie on the high mountainside.

There was, of course, little benevolence in the Aztec attitude to conquest, even if they practiced limited rather than total warfare. The eagerness with which neighboring city-states rallied to Cortés against the imperial forces shows plainly enough that they were hated. And no allies proved more loyal or helpful to the Spaniards than the Tlaxcalans, an unconquered people who for almost a century had been confronting the Aztecs in the most ritualized of all Mesoamerican military conflicts, the Flower Wars.

Dating to the earliest years of Aztec power, these stylized combats were fought by strictly observed rules. A battleground was chosen somewhere on the borders between the two combatant states, and a day was fixed in advance for the clash to begin. A large pyre of paper and incense set ablaze between the two armies signaled the onset of hostilities. The nature of the fighting was different from other battles, too; the fusillade of arrows, stones, and spears that began other conflicts was absent, for the point of the exercise was to demonstrate prowess in hand-to-hand combat.

The purpose of the Flower Wars seems to have been threefold. First—though this motive was never publicly acknowledged—they were a potent reminder of Aztec military might, discouraging potentially threatening neighbors from any more menacing demonstration of military enterprise. Second, they furnished an opportunity for combat training. Finally and perhaps most important, they provided a steady supply of prisoners of war to feed the Aztecs' unceasing need for sacrificial victims.

Human sacrifice had a part in most Mesoamerican cultures, but on nothing like the scale it was to assume under the Aztecs, for whom it drew its importance from the mystical significance attributed by them to blood, the vital fluid that kept the world running. Aztec creation myths were numerous and various, and often contradictory, but they all featured the deities' insatiable appetite for blood. One myth told how the sun had been created by a divine act of sacrifice. As the gods gathered in the primordial twilight, a malformed and diseased dwarf threw himself into an enormous brazier and rose from the coals transformed into the sun. For want of blood, however, the solar disk could not at first move through the sky. It was only after the other gods in turn had immolated themselves that the sun started on its daily course through the heavens; their deaths gave it life. From that time on, blood was needed to keep it on its course.

The blood of beasts was acceptable to the gods, and quails were sacrificed daily. In the temples, the day began with the beheading of the birds to salute the rising

WARRIORS' CLIFFSIDE RETREAT

Hidden in the mountains some 80 miles southwest of Tenochtitlan at a place called Malinalco *(right),* seven Aztec structures escaped destruction at the hands of 16th-century Spanish conquistadors. Hewn mostly from the living rock, though some were fronted with masonry, the structures apparently served the needs of two elite military cults, the Eagle and the Jaguar Knights. The most elaborate edifice, carved with eagle and jaguar motifs, can be seen with its restored conical thatched roof near the bottom of the aerial photograph. The building may have functioned both as a ceremonial center and as a secret setting for meetings of high-level Aztec leaders.

Some of the sacred stone sculptures resemble the Eagle Knight in a beaked helmet shown floating above the site. Only one of the wooden relics survives—a large cylindrical drum *(left).* Miraculously, it turned up intact in a nearby village, where the inhabitants had preserved it as evidence of their ancestors' once-glorious culture.

sun. The practice continued thereafter through the daylight hours; hundreds of quails died every day, necks wrung and heads torn off. Dogs, too, were sacrificed, at the winter solstice.

Humans were expected to offer their own blood. Few escaped this painful obligation; even babies had their ears pricked so that they might bleed. The ruler himself had to lacerate his flesh in the course of the coronation ceremony. In so doing he demonstrated an ability to endure pain that was expected of all Aztec males; the stoical indifference to suffering thus demonstrated was one gauge of a youth's suitability for advancement. The normal instrument of bloodletting was a maguey spine. The penitent would prick the upper ear, tongue, penis, or some other fleshy part of the body, then stick the bloody spike into a ball of plaited grass or place it on a bed of leaves.

The most diligent performers of self-laceration, however, were the priests. Besides the maguey-spine ritual, they would sometimes use obsidian blades to slice their earlobes or the foreskins of their penises; or they might pierce their flesh with obsidian skewers so they could insert straws to collect the blood. Apparently straws and thorns were also passed through holes in the tongue; some priests are said to have practiced this form of self-injury so energetically that they developed speech impediments. These seemingly masochistic exercises were thought to be beneficial for both the individual and the state, for the Aztecs conceived of a contractual relationship between men and gods; if sufficient offerings were made to them, the deities in return would provide rain, good harvests, and military success.

Yet self-laceration and animal sacrifice were not a sufficiently high price in themselves to ensure divine favor. Human sacrifice grew increasingly significant as the empire expanded. If any one man's hand can be seen behind the great upsurge in numbers killed, it seems

A jaguar skull, another relic of the Great Temple, clutches a jade ball between its teeth. With the ball serving symbolically as the animal's heart, the predator was thus assured an afterlife.

to have been that of Tlacaelel, the adviser to three rulers of Te-nochtitlan. In authority at a time when Aztec power was on the rise, he seems to have deliberately fostered the cult of Huitzilopochtli, with its attendant rites of sacrifice, as an imperialist creed and as a prop to encourage Aztec militarism. "In addition to being bold and cunning in the trickery of war," the Spanish chronicler Durán reported, he "also invented devilish, cruel, and frightful sacrifices."

According to Durán, Tlacaelel oversaw one monstrous sacrifice where the victims were so numerous that the Spaniard feared being called a liar for describing it, but, as he assured his readers, he had the information from reliable Aztec sources. "Before dawn the prisoners who were to be sacrificed were brought out and lined up in four files," he reported. "One extended from the foot of the steps to the pyramid all along the causeway that goes to Coyoacan and Xochimilco; it was almost one league in length. Another extended along the causeway of Guadalupe, and it was as long the first. The third went along the causeway of Tlacopan, and the fourth toward the east as far as the shore of the lagoon." It took four days for all the victims to be killed, and the streams of blood that ran down the temple steps were so great "that when they reached bottom and cooled they formed fat clots, enough to terrify one."

There were many different forms of human sacrifice, each associated with a given deity or one of the many festivals that punctuated the Aztec year, and the victims could be slaves as well as captured warriors. Without doubt the most common type of sacrifice was that in which the victim was held down while his still-pumping heart was cut out, but it was by no means the only method. Some unfortunates were decapitated. Still others became living targets, shot through with arrows or atlatl darts.

Perhaps the noblest form of human sacrifice was one that involved gladiatorial combat, albeit of a lopsided kind. Known as the Flaying of Men, it formed part of a ritual carried out in the spring, the time of planting, and celebrated the rejuvenation of life. The prisoners, seized on the battlefield and brought back to Tenochtitlan, were carefully tended by their captors and treated almost as kinsmen, as brethren in death, that they might honor the victors through the dignity and bravery of their dying. Indeed, this relationship started on the battlefield where, by tradition, the warrior was supposed to say to his prisoner, "He is as my beloved son," and the prisoner in turn was to reply, "He is as my beloved father."

103

The rite of the Flaying of Men took place over a two-day period at the temple of the god Xipe Totec, known as the Flayed One or the Flayer, whose connections with the east, a region considered by the Aztecs to be a land of plenty, made him an appropriate deity to please at this time of year. The ceremony called for the prisoners, wearing paper loincloths, to be smeared all over with a chalky substance. Then their heads were covered with sticky latex, the juice of the rubber tree, to which turkey feathers were attached; the milky-colored latex was applied to their faces as well. On the first day of the rite, only the lesser captives went to their deaths atop Xipe's temple; they were supposed to sprint up the steps, but many had to be dragged to the sacrificial stone by the temple priests. After they had their hearts cut out, their lifeless bodies were thrown down the steps and flayed and butchered. One thigh of each was dispatched to the ruler, while the victims' captors got to keep the rest except for the heads, which were used to decorate an enormous skull rack.

The warriors now summoned their kinsmen to their homes for ritual cannibal feasts. Mindful that they themselves might wind up one day on an enemy's killing stone, they abjured their captives' flesh, but urged their relatives to each eat a small piece with a handful of uncooked corn kernels—a symbolic act calling to mind the earth's bounty. With much wailing and weeping for the deaths that might one day befall their own sons, either on the battleground or as sacrifices, the families partook of the flesh and corn.

The next day, the more important prisoners were sacrificed on the so-called gladiatorial stone at the base of Xipe Totec's pyramid. The captives had been prepared for the rite over a four-day period during which, among other things, they were obliged to fight in mock combat and submit to a sham removal of their hearts—that organ being represented by dried corn kernels. After spending the eve of their deaths with their captors, who symbolically cut off their warlocks at midnight, they were led to the temple. The high priest, dressed as Xipe, came down the steps, followed by his entourage.

A captive would be tethered to the waist-high, circular stone, which was set on a raised platform. Stripped to his loincloth, he was provided with mock

104

Religious sacrifice took a variety of forms in Aztec culture. The remains of dozens of small bodies found at the Great Temple (above) *are testimony to the practice of sacrificing children, in the belief that their tears brought rain. At the opposite end of the spectrum, warriors ritually pricked themselves with maguey spines and bled into a grass ball, sometimes placed in a* cuauhxicalli, *or eagle vessel* (left).

arms—four pine cudgels and a club rimmed with feathers in place of the usual obsidian blades. With these imitation weapons he was expected to defend himself against four of the mightiest Eagle and Jaguar Knights, who were armed with real weapons. To ease his pain he was given a drink of pulque, spiked, doubtless with a drug prepared from morning-glory seeds, and then he was set upon by his adversaries and their superior weapons.

As he fought his losing battle, he was subjected to what was known as the striping, the slitting here and there of his skin, so that his blood would seep from the tiny wounds. There was perhaps an intended parallel here, the breaking of the skin suggesting the splitting open of seeds in the earth as they germinate. When at last the poor captive collapsed, the high priest impersonating Xipe stepped forward, cut out the heart, raised it up to the sun as an offering, and then dipped a hollow cane into the pool of blood rising in the chest cavity and held it up so that the sun might drink. He presented the captor with the cane and a bowl of the blood with which the warrior went about the city, reddening the mouths of the idols in the temples.

After making his rounds, the warrior returned to Xipe's temple and rejoined the celebrants, who flayed and dismembered the captives; they then lubricated their own naked bodies with grease and slipped into the skin. Sometimes a warrior would pass the honor of wearing a skin to a penitent. Trailing blood and grease, the gruesomely clad men ran through the city, "thus terrifying those they followed," as Sahagún noted. They would chase youths so bold as to try to pluck at the navels to get a little of the dead men's skin under their fingernails and would beat any they caught. Welcomed everywhere, they went from house to house. According to Sahagún, they took seats spread with leaves, and "their hosts provided them with necklaces formed of maize ears; they placed garlands of flowers upon their shoulders; they placed crowns of flowers upon their heads."

The second-day's rite also included a cannibal feast for each warrior's family, and as on the day before, the slayer would hold back from eating the flesh, saying aloud, "Shall I perchance eat my very self?" During the 20-day period in which he wore the skin, he and those around him had to endure the stench it gave off. In the end, he shed the crumbling, rotting suit, which was buried in a cave at the foot of Xipe's temple, then cleansed himself deeply, rubbing off any lingering grease with cornmeal. The ceremony over, the reborn spring was joyously celebrated throughout the city.

Women were sacrificed at a fall festival honoring the mother goddesses of growing and ripe maize, the Aztec staple. They were decapitated, their heads lopped off like ears of corn as they danced in imitation of the divinity. The idea of divine impersonation was taken furthest in the case of the handsome youth chosen annually to represent Tezcatlipoca, archsorcerer and supreme god of the Aztec pantheon. For a year the young man was honored as an incarnation of the deity, walking about in the apparel associated with the god and playing on the flute. One month before his death, he was provided with four maidens representing goddesses to enjoy. When the appointed day arrived, he had to say farewell to them and climb the steps of the temple alone, casting down and breaking a flute on each step as he ascended. Then the waiting priests seized him and cut out his heart. A new youth was immediately chosen to take his place for the following year until his time too should come.

Children were offered to Tlaloc, the god of rain and agricultural fertility. The victims were bought from their parents; Aztec records indicate that infants with two cowlicks of hair, born on days considered propitious, were sought, and that the price paid was high. Their fate was reported by Durán. Each spring "the entire nobility of the land, kings and princes, and

Known as the Tomb of Time, an altar decorated with skulls and bones served as the burial place of each passing century in Tenochtitlan. Every 52 years a bundle of 52 canes—the number of years in an Aztec century—was thrust through the opening on top in a symbolic interment.

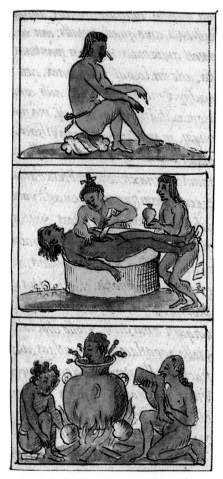

In an illustration from the Florentine Codex prepared by Friar Sahagún, a sacrificial victim tearfully contemplates his fate before a priest cuts out his heart, after which two Aztecs boil and consume his body in an act of ritual cannibalism.

great lords, took a child of six or seven years and placed him within an enclosed litter so that he would not be seen." The procession crossed Lake Tetzcoco and wended its way to the summit of Mount Tlaloc, a peak near Tenochtitlan that the Mexicans associated with clouds and rain. "If they go along crying," an Aztec document preserved in another chronicle records, "if their tears keep flowing, if their tears keep falling, it was said, indeed it will rain." At Mount Tlaloc the child was sacrificed by the priests to the wail of trumpets, conch shells, and flutes, and its blood was used to bathe an image of the god; if a drought persisted, additional children might be killed. Little wonder that the memory of the ceremony was slow to die even after the Spanish conquest.

Meanwhile, in Tenochtitlan itself, a little girl dressed in blue, the color of water, waited in a second enclosed litter within the Great Temple precinct. When news came through that the mountain sacrifice had been accomplished, she was carried to a canoe and paddled to a given spot out on the lake. There her throat was slit, so that her blood flowed into the water, and her body was cast into the lake.

The saddest discovery at the Great Temple was made in late July 1980, on the northwest corner of the side of the pyramid dedicated to Tlaloc. Digging revealed a cache containing stone vessels bearing Tlaloc's effigy laid on top of the bones of 42 of his young victims. Evidence from dental examination of the skulls suggested that the children were between three and seven years of age at the time of their deaths. Half showed some signs of disease, raising the possibility that children in poor health may have formed a disproportionate percentage of the victims; evidence from similar caches of bones excavated at nearby Tlatelolco seems to confirm this finding. Medical examination of the skeletons suggested that the children died by having their throats cut rather than their hearts extracted. It was not possible to determine whether they were boys or girls.

Just as sacrifices to Tlaloc involved water and tears, so those to Xiuhtecuhutli, the fire god, featured burning. His partially drugged victims were tossed into braziers and roasted on the coals. Before they could expire, however, their blistered bodies were pulled out by priests equipped with hooks, so the chests could be opened and the hearts removed. Some were dispatched by drowning or strangulation; others were crushed against a rock or locked up and left to die miserably.

One of the strangest sacrificial rites was the merchants' custom of offering up so-called bathed slaves. A merchant would buy an attractive slave, male or female, who was skilled in the arts of singing and dancing. He would build houses in which his purchase would later be expected to dance. He would make lavish gifts to other merchants and military men who had already sacrificed slaves of their own, and would go on pilgrimage to the merchant headquarters of Tochtepec, near Mexico's east coast, to indicate his intention of partaking in the slave-bathing ceremony. Returning to Tenochtitlan, he would embark on a lavish round of entertaining at which the chosen slave, who had been meanwhile well cared for, would perform, bedecked in fine clothes and ornaments.

The process culminated in an elaborate set of rites whose climax came when master and servant climbed the staircase of the Great Temple together. At the top, the merchant handed the slave over to the priests, who cut out his heart. The body was then returned to the merchant, to be consumed by his relatives at a banquet. "Separately, in an *olla*, they cooked the grains of maize," the chronicler Sahagún reported. "They served his flesh on it. They placed only a little on top of it. No chili did they add to it; they only sprinkled salt on it. Indeed all the host's kinsmen ate of it." Thus merchants won status and showed off their success.

The cannibalism that often followed Aztec sacrifice was governed by strict rules. Because sacrificial victims were thought to have become divine, their limbs were consecrated and were, in the words of a chronicler, "eaten with reverence, ritual, and fastidiousness—as if it were something from heaven." The torsos, however, were treated with less respect, serving as meat for the wild animals in the royal zoo.

In many cases, sacrificial victims apparently went stoically to their deaths, convinced a glorious afterlife with the gods awaited them. There are accounts of warriors captured in battle insisting on being sacrificed even when offered their freedom, though whether the motive was religious credulity, the wish to display manly indifference to unbearable pain, or the desire to escape the shame of defeat is impossible to tell.

In the end, the blood-hungry gods let the invincible Aztecs down. More than five centuries after the last victim died atop the Great Temple, the words of a poet ring achingly hollow: "Proud of itself is the city of Mexico-Tenochtitlan. Here no one fears to die in war. That is our glory. Who could conquer Tenochtitlan? Who could shake the foundation of heaven?"

THE TEMPLE OF DEATH

We shall conquer all the people in the universe," boasted Huitzilopochtli, patron god of the Aztecs—or at least that is what the Aztecs reported his having said to them. And that was not his only prophecy: "I will make you lords and kings of every place in the world." In fulfillment of their god-given destiny, the Aztecs designated the center of their power with the utmost exactitude. At the intersection of the causeways leading to their island capital of Tenochtitlan, they erected an imposing four-tiered pyramid that the Spaniards would call *el Templo Mayor,* or the Great Temple.

Like a spike through the fabric of existence, this man-made mountain was seen as joining the everyday terrestrial plane to the heavens above and the underworld below. Fittingly, it was a fearsome place. At its base crawled immense stone snakes. Within the structure lay dark chambers stuffed with religious offerings—figurines, stone masks, animal bones, seashells, skulls. Two steep sets of stairs led up the western face to the pair of shrines that held the statues of Huitzilopochtli, god of sun and war, and Tlaloc, god of water and fertility. Here, to ensure that crops flourished and tribute continued to flow from subject peoples, priests

carried out a regular round of sacrifical rites, tearin[g] the hearts of male victims *(above)*, most of whom [were] captives or slaves.

When the Spaniards seized Tenochtitlan, [they] sought to erase every trace of the alien gods. The[y tore] down stones of the sacred mountain and used th[em to] build a cathedral; apparently they removed an[d de]stroyed the effigies of Huitzilopochtli and Tla[loc,] although some people believe that the Indians sna[tched] them away and hid them. But the soft subsoil o[f Te]nochtitlan retained secrets that would come to [light] centuries later. In 1978, when workers laying elec[tric] cable near the center of Mexico City discovered a [rem]nant of the Great Temple—the huge stone portr[ait of] Coyolxauhqui, the dismembered rebellious sist[er of] Huitzilopochtli—a new era of Mexican archae[ology] opened. For the next five years, archaeologists and [oth]er specialists excavated the surrounding area. [They] learned that the edifice razed by the Spaniards ha[d been] only an outer shell, one version of the Aztec w[orld] center built over the structures of earlier temples. [Hid]den in the spongy soil into which these had gra[dually] sunk was a prodigious record of Aztec belief writt[en on] the Great Temple's blood-soaked stones.

Soon after the Aztecs settled at Tenochtitlan in AD 1325, they gave thanks for their deliverance to their guardian deity by fashioning a shrine from reeds, straw, and grass. This rude structure—long since decayed—was the seed from which the Great Temple grew. Over the next two centuries it would be repeatedly rebuilt, each new version enclosing the one before. Meanwhile, a vast ceremonial precinct spread around the temple—a walled area where worshipers, entering through four gates oriented to the four cardinal points, propitiated a multitude of gods at as many as 78 temples and shrines.

In this sacred setting, the Great Temple rose in a pyramid some 135 feet high, with more than a hundred steps ascending to the sacrificial area on top. As archaeologists dug deeper at the site, they traced at least six reconstructions. Some of the rebuilding had been done because the increasingly heavy structure steadily sank into the waterlogged earth, but much of the work was designed to reflect the growth of empire. A diplomatic message from a neighboring state delivered to the Aztec ruler during one phase of enlargement urged, "Make it your destiny to see that the honor of the Aztecs does not diminish but rather becomes greater." Each completed expansion demanded celebrations that were deemed sure to please the gods, including mass sacrifices that could continue for days on end.

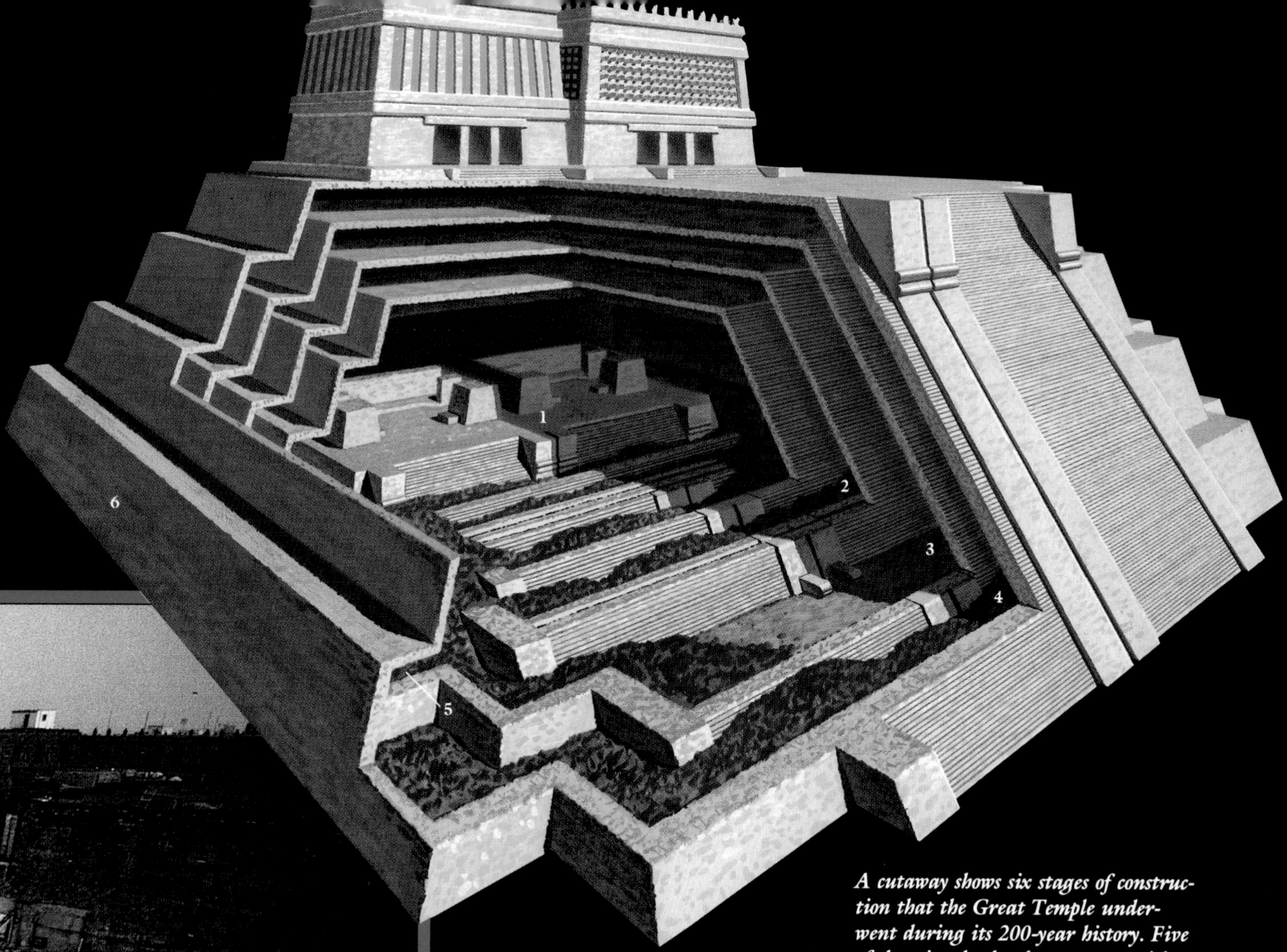

A cutaway shows six stages of construction that the Great Temple underwent during its 200-year history. Five of these involved enlargements, with new walls laid over old ones and rubble used to fill in the spaces. The overhead view reveals excavated areas that yielded significant finds, including the Coyolxauhqui stone.

Stage I (unexcavated)
1 Stage II (ca. 1428)
2 Stage III (1431)
3 Stage IV (ca. 1454-1469)
4 Stage V (ca. 1480)
5 Stage VI (ca. 1500)
6 Stage VII (ca. 1502-1520)

Close by Mexico City's cathedral, the Great Temple ruins embrace a 7,000-square-yard area. Sacrificical victims climbed, danced, or were led up the steps to the killing stones once positioned on the long-vanished top.

111

The Aztecs' view of life was at once optimistic and pessimistic: All that the gods provided the gods could take away, especially in Mexico. Here the rainy season was followed by a dry one in which plants could wither and die. Indeed, the Aztecs, who had wandered through arid lands for years before settling down, had firsthand experience of the disaster drought could bring. Twice they had endured severe famines. Out of such calamity, they saw the world as existing in a state of precarious balance that could shift and result in cataclysm. In an effort to stave off disaster, they regularly propitiated the gods with blood.

As the excavation of the Great Temple proceeded, the archaeologists uncovered more and more evidence of Aztec devotion, but none more chilling, perhaps, than the remains of a shrine to Huitzilopochtli. There they came face to face with the dark stone opposite, over which priests had stretched victims and cut out their hearts. At Tlaloc's shrine nearby they found the sculpture below, thought to represent a messenger between the god and the priests. It may have been used as an altar or offertory for the steaming hearts that the Aztecs believed would help ensure Tlaloc's blessing.

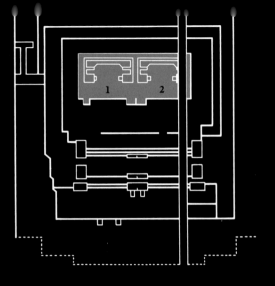

Still retaining traces of its original paint, a divine intermediary, or chac-mool, *reclines near Tlaloc's shrine, eternally awaiting bloody offerings.*

One version of the Great Temple—the first great remodeling, designated Stage II—was unearthed almost intact. The darker area shows where the supine figure (1) and sacrificial stone (2) pictured below turned up.

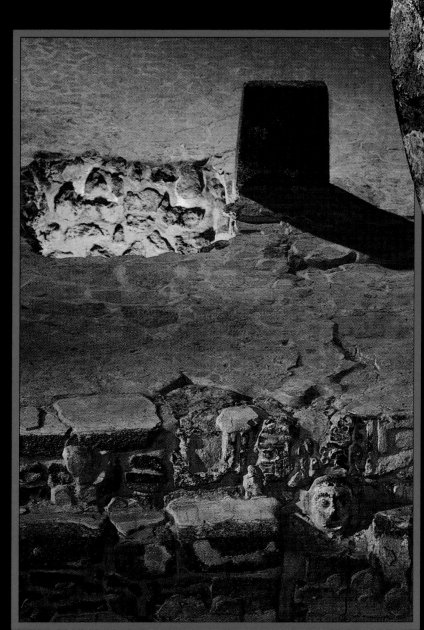

The sacrificial stone in Huitzilopoch-tli's shrine presents a grim profile. Victims had their hearts cut out here with ritual knives like the one above, shown actual size. Breaking through the floor beside the stone, the excavators found several knives that had been left as religious offerings.

PROBING THE TEMPLE'S SECRETS

Dreadful indeed were the two deities who resided atop the Great Temple. "Huitzilopochtli," reported one Spanish writer, "was a second Hercules, who was extremely strong and very bellicose, a great destroyer of towns and slayer of people." Tlaloc, who supplied the rains that made the earth productive, had his fierce side, too. He "sent hail and lightning and storms and danger on rivers and at sea," said this same chronicler.

The Great Temple embodies the gods' dual control in many ways—most prominently in their two shrines, but also in associated sculptures, such as those shown below. The pyramid itself is a double symbol, representing both the holy mountain where Huitzilopochtli was born and the heavens where Tlaloc's rains formed.

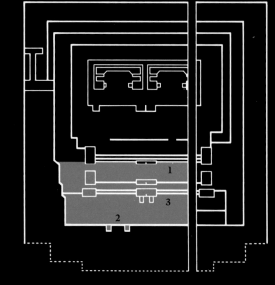

Numbers on this highlighted floor plan note the places where the objects in the photographs turned up during digging. The standing figures (1), the frogs (2), and the sacrificial stone (3) date to the Stage III reconstruction of the temple, begun in 1431.

Sitting on pedestals in front of stairs leading to Tlaloc's shrine, a pair of frogs symbolize earth, water, and fertility. They were also associated with the underworld, since they burrowed in mud during the dry season.

Found reclining against the stairway that rose to Huitzilopochtli's shrine, these nearly life-size statues, referred to as standard-bearers, may represent the war god's brothers. They are thought to have adorned the summit.

114

GIFTS FOR THE INSATIABLE GODS

As archaeologists explored the various generations of the Great Temple, they found much that successive reconstructions had hidden from view even in Aztec times. In and around the temple were more than 80 caches of offerings to the gods. The repositories contained more than 7,000 items, ranging from skulls of sacrificed infants to seashells. In some cases, the articles had been placed in stone chambers; others were sealed in stone caskets, and some had been hidden in the rubble behind walls.

Only a small fraction of these propitiatory gifts are of Aztec origin; most come from tribute-paying areas, testimony to the scope and strength of the Aztec empire. The caches hold many effigies of gods, particularly of Tlaloc. The secret troves also include masks, funerary urns, flint and obsidian blades, jaguar skeletons, crocodile heads, rattlesnake and boa skins, and turtle shells, as well as a large array of corals.

Within the offertory chambers, the articles were evidently arranged according to some ritualistic system, but the meaning of the placement patterns has not yet been deciphered. There is no doubt, however, that the gifts were a kind of metaphoric language for the pillars of the Aztec world: images of their gods, the spoils of war, and the natural abundance of the earth.

A chamber of offerings built into the temple when it was enlarged between 1469 and 1481 holds painted jars, stone masks, jaguar bones, 11 multicolored effigies of Tlaloc, and the skulls, ribs, and limb bones of 30 babies and children, none older than eight years. All the objects here are seen just as they lay when archaeologists found them.

This Olmec mask, more than two millennia old when it was placed in a cache of offerings at the Great Temple, measures a little over four inches high.

The fierce face of Tlaloc, his eye rings formed of coiled serpents, glares from the base of a multicolored vase—a receptacle symbolizing the water that brought forth the bounty of the soil.

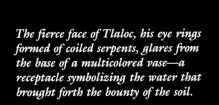

A group of tiny fish, carved from mother-of-pearl by an Aztec craftsman, honors Tlaloc, who held dominion over the world's seas, lakes, and rivers as well as the clouds that provided farmers with rain.

TREASURES FROM THE TEMPLE'S DEPTHS

Whenever the Great Temple underwent an expansion, offerings from subject peoples were lavished on its resident gods. One chronicler of Aztec history reported: "Each city, striving to surpass the others, arrived with its jewels and precious stones to throw them into the foundations. They threw in so much treasure that it was an astonishing thing; and the Aztecs said that their Huitzilopochtli had given them those riches, so it was appropriate that they be dedicated to his service, since they truly belonged to him." The homage, whether paid to Huitzilopochtli or to Tlaloc, came from all the outlying regions—indeed, from every corner of the empire.

A great sweep of time as well as space was represented by the gifts. Into temple caches went masks made 1,000 years earlier in the city of Teotihuacan, the place where, according to Aztec lore, the fifth sun was born. The oldest offering of all was an Olmec mask created around 800 BC. Perhaps such gifts were intended to link the Aztecs to these illustrious cultures of the distant past, helping to justify their right to hold dominion over all other groups.

Symbol of life, creation, and fecundity, a nearly three-foot-long conch carved from stone once occupied a prominent place in the temple. Excavators uncovered it where the Indians had apparently hidden it from the Spaniards.

With flints inserted in its nasal cavity and mouth, and bone and pyrite plugging its eye sockets, a human skull conjures the horror of death. The holes in the brow may have been threaded so it could be worn as a mask.

A COMPLEMENTARY TRIO OF SHRINES

Around the year 1500, the Aztecs were hard-pressed to maintain a firm grip on their empire, but difficulties in war and governance did not stand in the way of yet another expansion of the Great Temple; indeed, the troubles may have made enlargement seem even more urgent.

During this phase of rebuilding, designated Stage VI, three small temples were constructed in a flagstone court on the north side of the pyramid. One was a rectangular, east-facing structure that enclosed a round altar; nearby stood a large sculpture of a deity thought to be Huehueteotl—the old fire god *(below)*. A second shrine contained a small, undecorated altar. The third shrine was a macabre platform adorned with 240 carvings of skulls *(opposite, far right)*. It is thought that priests may have placed the heads of sacrificial victims here after decapitation.

Hunched and fanged, this stone effigy of the old fire god has a flat top so that it could hold a brazier containing burning incense, used during Great Temple ceremonies.

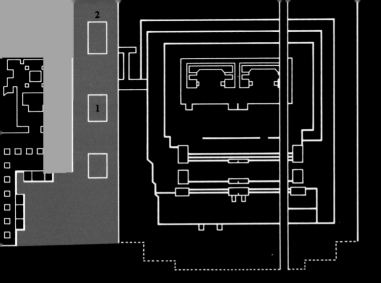

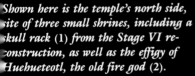

Shown here is the temple's north side, site of three small shrines, including a skull rack (1) from the Stage VI reconstruction, as well as the effigy of Huehueteotl, the old fire god (2).

Stone skulls, originally covered with coats of stucco, are arrayed on three sides of an altar meant to recall the racks on which the Aztecs displayed the heads of their sacrificial victims.

THE HALL OF THE EAGLE KNIGHTS

Warriors as well as priests honored the gods at the Great Temple, as is evidenced by the archaeologists' discovery of a three-chambered hall close by. Here the most accomplished soldiers of the noble class—members of a military order associated with the eagle—gathered for their rites. Altars, statues, and braziers found at the site testify to their ancient ceremonies, as does a frieze depicting the eagle warriors in plumed headdresses and centering on a spiked symbol for the personal bloodletting expected of them. In effigy, at least, members of the long-ago military order were still on hand when archaeologists cleared the hall: A pair of life-size statues of these heroic men dressed in full eagle regalia stood guard at the entrance to the second chamber.

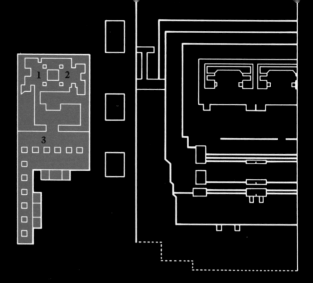

The Hall of the Eagle Knights, dating from Stage VI, lay in the courtyard on the Great Temple's north side, demarcated here, with locations of the Tlaloc brazier (1), the skeleton (2), and the eagle warrior figure (3) shown.

Among the statues in the Hall of the Eagle Knights was this now-headless ceramic skeleton—thought to represent Mictlantecuhtli, god of the dead. His bones poke through his flesh, suggesting the ephemeral nature of life.

Uncovered within one of the chambers of the Hall of the Eagle Knights, a pottery representation of the god Tlaloc weeping tears of rain served as a brazier used in the ceremonies.

As though ready to
Knight wearing a

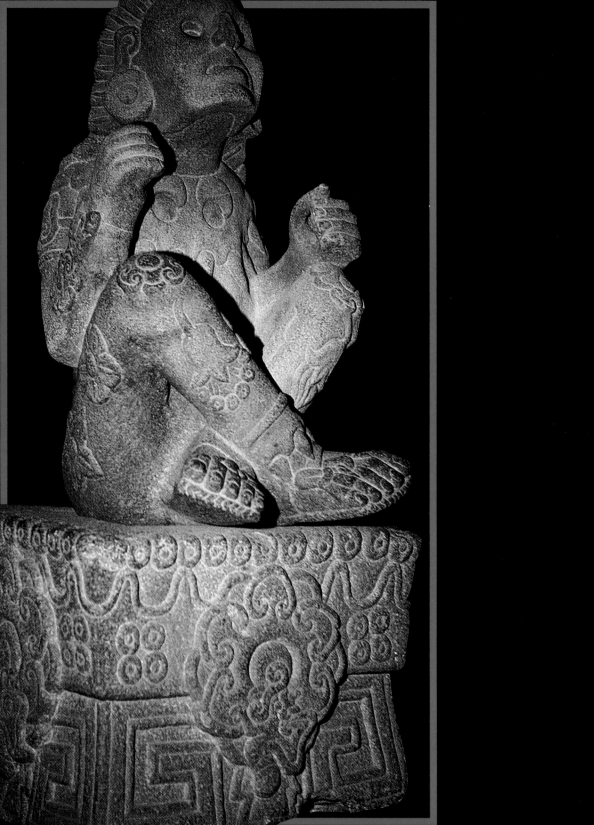

THE GENTLER SIDE OF AZTEC LIFE

Given their fierce reputation, Aztec warriors looked forward to a curious fate after death—one that perhaps says more about their culture's sensibilities than the gruesome rites performed at the Great Temple. According to the Florentine Codex, warriors who died in battle traveled straightaway to the Eastern Paradise to become attendants of the sun, "the turquoise prince." Before dawn each morning, they would gather on a vast plain to await the sun's arrival, which they greeted with relish, beating their wooden clubs against their shields in noisy celebration. Dancing and singing, they would then escort the sun to its zenith, where women who had died in childbirth—a battle of another sort—would take over, transporting the fiery orb on a feathered litter to the day's end.

But an even more blissful reward lay in store. After four years as "companions of the sun," the souls of Aztec fighting men returned to earth, "changed into precious birds—hummingbirds, orioles, yellow birds, and chalky butterflies. And here they came to suck honey from the various flowers."

No image better conjures up the startling contradictions inherent in the Aztec world: tough, death-inured warriors transformed into hummingbirds and butterflies. In many aspects of their daily lives, the Aztecs exemplified such competing strains. Their propen-

125

sity for bloodletting was offset by a deep-seated reverence for beauty in both nature and the arts, their excesses reined in by a rigorous social order and code of ethics. Theirs was, in fact, a complex and diverse society that, like so many others throughout history, was as fascinating in its ordinary comings and goings as in its grandest and its most horrific moments.

Fundamental to the culture was a love of language. The Aztecs deservedly rank among the world's great speechmakers, seizing virtually every opportunity to flaunt their rhetorical skills. At public and private functions alike, Aztec speakers engaged in elaborate recitations of historical events or legends of the ancestors and the gods. Stories passed orally from generation to generation; a number of works of literature—ranging from poems to myths—have survived, written down in the years following the Spanish conquest by converts to Catholicism who had learned the European alphabet.

Some orations may have bored their listeners, especially when one of the old men chose to preach from the so-called *Precepts of the Elders,* a lengthy cataloging of advice and admonition intended to keep the younger generation versed in proper behavior. But this would have been rare. Jacques Soustelle, a French scholar who devoted his life to studying the Aztecs, has noted that public occasions could turn into "positive tournaments of eloquence," with speakers—not just men, but noble women also—exercising their talents for wordplay and the clever use of metaphor. A standard technique was to unite two words or phrases to express an abstract concept. Taken together, for example, the words for "jade" and "feathers" meant "beauty." The language itself, Nahuatl, noted to this day for its melodiousness, added to the effect; *Nahuatl* translates as "elegant speech."

Against a backdrop of a watery city, the Aztec marketplace swarms with activity in the well-known Mexican painter Diego Rivera's 1945 mural, The Great City of Tenochtitlan. *The variety of products pictured—including featherwork and baskets of multicolored corn—along with busy merchants, porters in forehead straps, and even a prostitute raising her skirt, brings to life the colorful reports of Spanish conquistadors who witnessed the thriving entrepôt at Tlatelolco.*

By far the highest form of the art was poetry—"poetry" being designated in Nahuatl by the pairing of the words for "flower" and "song." Poets were among the most respected figures in the society, so much so that they would not hesitate to name themselves in their works. Noblemen and even rulers would sometimes try their hand at composition; among the most famous practitioners was Nezahualcoyotl, leader of the Tetzcocans, whose verses were still being sung decades after his death in 1472.

Not unlike their modern counterparts, Aztec poets often chose as their theme the evanescence of beauty and the suffering of the artist: "Eagerly does my heart yearn for flowers; I suffer with songs, yet I create them on earth, I, Cuacuauhtzin: I crave flowers that will not perish in my hands! Where might I find lovely flowers, lovely songs? Such as I seek, spring does not produce on earth."

The importance of language grew as the society matured. In the decades leading up to the arrival of the Spaniards, a deft tongue had become one of the emblems of authority, and quality and refinement of speech set off the classes from one another. Aztec rulers traditionally bore two honorific titles: *tlacatecuhtli,* "lord of men," and *huey tlatoani,* "great speaker." Motecuhzoma II, like his predecessors, depended on military prowess as a basis of his power; yet his effectiveness as an orator, especially before the ruling council made up of state officials, priests, and warriors, clearly helped him to maintain his position at the center of the Aztec government.

As for the common people, they exercised their love of speech in several venues, but in no more colorful a setting than the economic heart of this bustling society. North of the Great Temple, in the adjacent city of Tlatelolco, which Tenochtitlan had annexed, lay a market that surpassed any the invading Spaniards had ever seen. From it rose a great din as people went about the daily business of bartering. In his second letter back to his monarch, Charles V, Cortés ran on at length about the place and all it held. Although he felt that he had not done it justice, leaving out many items he could not remember or had not been able to identify, his account captures a sense of the astounding variety of goods. "There is also one square twice as big as that of Salamanca," he wrote, "with arcades all around, where more than 60,000 people come each day to buy and sell, and where every kind of merchandise produced in these lands is found; provisions as well as ornaments of gold and silver, lead, brass, copper, tin, stones, shells, bones, and feathers. They also sell lime, hewn and unhewn stone, adobe bricks, tiles, and cut and uncut woods of various kinds." The remarkable abundance of food available on any market day might include corn, beans, salt, honey, chili peppers, tomatoes, various fruits, edible roots, nuts, fish, frogs, and insect eggs, which were treasured as a delicacy.

The temple plaza of Tlatelolco—shown partly excavated amid its modern surroundings—flourished as a center of religious and ceremonial life next-door to its sister city, Tenochtitlan. Just beyond the plaza, crowds gathered in a vast marketplace: the commercial hub of the empire.

A wide range of fowl and game was commonly bought and sold. "There is a street where they sell game and birds of every species found in this land," Cortés reported, "turkeys, partridges and quails, wild ducks, flycatchers, widgeons, turtledoves, pigeons, cane birds, parrots, eagles and eagle owls, falcons, sparrow hawks and kestrels; and they sell the skins of some of these birds of prey with their feathers, heads, and claws. They sell rabbits and hares, and stags and small gelded dogs, which they breed for eating."

People flocked to Tlatelolco for practically all their needs. At barbers' stalls, patrons could be shaved or have their hair washed. Other booths sold decorated gourds, obsidian mirrors, and cosmetics. Cortés was impressed by the array of medicinal herbs and roots as well compounds, ointments, and plasters prepared in apothecaries' shops. Love potions were available as well, along with other ingredients for working magic. Elsewhere, household items such as earthenware cooking pots, wooden bowls, reed mats, brooms, and baskets were stacked high.

The section devoted to clothing must have been particularly impressive. Here, everything from the skins of wild animals and fancy embroidered capes and skirts to rough cloth and maguey-thread fabrics for everyday dress was available. The shops were undoubtedly among the most colorful in the entire square. "There are many sorts of spun cotton," Cortés noted, "in hanks of every color, and it seems like the silk market at Granada, except here there is a much greater quantity." For brilliance of hues their only rival would have been the booths of artists' supplies, where there were "as many colors for painters as may be found in Spain."

However crowded and busy it may have been, the market was noteworthy for its orderliness. Bernal Díaz, Cortés's soldier-chronicler, was astonished not only at the overall spectacle but also at "the method and regularity of everything." The square was divided into separate shopping districts for each category of goods or services. All items were sold by quantity or by some other measure such as length, but, as far as Cortés could see, never by weight. Coins and paper money did not exist, but a few selected commodities served as currency. The standard medium of exchange was cacao beans, although mantles or cloaks called *cuachtli* were also frequently used. One hundred cacao beans were the equivalent of one cuachtli—and both were enough to buy a dugout canoe or 100 sheets of bark paper. Two cuachtli bought a load of cochineal, a red dye derived from an insect. Still-more-expensive articles such as a warrior's costume and shield, a feather cloak, or jewelry called for mantles, small copper ax blades, or gold dust. Thirty mantles purchased a slave; 40, one who could sing and dance.

As the people wandered up and down the many aisles of stalls, they would chat with one another as well as barter with the vendors. Occasionally, voices might be raised in anger when someone suspected that a seller had cheated or was charging an exorbitant price. Settling such disputes with all haste seems to have been a prime concern. According to Cortés: "There is in this great square a very large building like a courthouse, where 10 or 12 persons sit as judges. They preside over all that happens in the markets and sentence criminals. There are in this square other persons who walk among the people to see what they are selling and the measures they are using; and they have been seen to break some that were false."

These arbiters of justice for the marketplace came from a distinct social group known as the *pochteca,* or professional traders. The name referred not to the generalized mass of hawkers, peddlers, and stallkeepers of the market but to the traveling merchants who conducted the lucrative foreign trade with the so-called Hot Lands to the southeast. The economy's chief powerbrokers, they were just one step below the ruling nobility. A people very much unto themselves, they lived in their own separate districts of the city, married only within their own class, and worshiped their own god—Yacate-cuhtli, the "lord who guides."

Within their class, the pochteca were as stratified as the society at large, and ritual played as important a role in their endeavors. Ten cities within the Aztec confederacy had their own pochteca corporations, typically managed by a handful of older merchants who no longer ventured out on trading expeditions. Caravans were led by the *tecuhnenenque,* or traveling lords, experienced traders who had distinguished themselves on dangerous missions in the past. Young apprentices, perhaps on their first journey, would accompany them to learn the ins and outs of dealing with foreigners. Because of the perils likely to be encountered from gangs of robbers along the way, certain of the traders would be armed; these were either the *tecyaua-louanime,* "those who surround the enemy," or the even more fearsome *tecuanime,* "the wild beasts." In addition to protecting the

A WARRIOR-KING WHO NURTURED ART, POETRY, AND GOOD GOVERNMENT

Nezahualcoyotl, often called today the poet-king of Tetzcoco, a neighboring city-state of Tenochtitlan, ushered in an age of intellectual achievement for his people. He ruled according to lofty principles developed during his youth. As a teenager, he saw his father killed by invaders and spent the following eight years as a virtual exile. Hiding from his enemies for the last two years in the mountains, he received aid from Aztec allies, and in battle won the throne that rightfully belonged to him.

As ruler, Nezahualcoyotl became a renowned poet; he was also a patron of art and science and sponsored public recitals of verse. He built a temple without idols dedicated to a single deity, "the unknown god," and banned human sacrifice there. Wandering anonymously among his people, Nezahualcoyotl would reward worthy citizens and redress grievances.

A 16th-century illustration shows Nezahualpilli, son of Nezahualcoyotl, who ascended the throne at seven and reigned for 44 years, during which time he advanced his father's high ideals. His flowers, sandals, and long decorative cotton mantle signify his elevated rank.

Poised to lunge, Nezahualcoyotl grips his obsidian-studded club and raises his leather shield. In battle, he signaled his men with the drum on his back. The gold lip plug was worn as a sign of status.

THE GARDEN PARADISE OF TETZCOTZINGO

At the foot of the Sacred Hill of Tetzcotzingo (*far right*), some six miles east of his capital, Nezahualcoyotl built an elaborate country villa. Terracing the adjoining mountain, he turned its arid slopes into lush gardens, watered by numerous pools and canals.

Paths led up to the 180-foot-high summit, where a ritual area lay. Baths, probably for religious purification, were located at key points along the way. Like all the gardens' waterworks, they drew from a stone aqueduct that was connected to springs atop Mount Tlaloc, several peaks away.

Although church officials destroyed the buildings and sculpture in 1539, archaeologists studying the site, as well as early texts and illustrations, discovered clues to the gardens' original appearance. A mask of Tlaloc, the rain god, engraved on bedrock, indicated that there was a Tlaloc temple on the summit. Just below the crest were found remnants of a large rock that once had listed, in glyphs, the king's achievements. Nearby, a stone stump proved to be the remnant of a sculpted plumed coyote, Nezahualcoyotl's animal namesake and totem. And on an overlook facing Lake Tetzcoco lay fragments of a shrine to earth and agricultural deities.

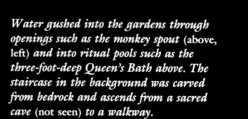

Water gushed into the gardens through openings such as the monkey spout (above, left) and into ritual pools such as the three-foot-deep Queen's Bath above. The staircase in the background was carved from bedrock and ascends from a sacred cave (not seen) to a walkway.

QUEEN'S BATH

A topographical map of the garden notes ritual baths (circles) on a path (red) with canals (blue), fed by an aqueduct. The trail winds past remainders of sacred sites (squares), including earth and agricultural deities (1), a Tlaloc mask (2), and various historical monuments (3).

caravan, they might also help persuade reluctant communities to accept Aztec terms. On the longest treks, which could last for several years and might reach as far as present-day Panama, the *nahualoztomeca,* or disguised traders, played a crucial role. They could speak the languages of remote peoples and would dress in their garb to act as spies, ferreting out the most promising opportunities.

Careful preparations were necessary for a major expedition. The Aztec goods that would be traded for exotic foreign items had to be assembled and then divvied out to porters, who would be expected to carry the heavy loads and walk as much as 30 to 40 miles a day. Due consideration was also given to ceremony. The chiefs of the corporation would consult divinatory almanacs to help select the most propitious date for setting out. The day before departure, offerings were presented to Yacatecuhtli and to other gods, and a feast was given for the travelers. Ritual speeches emphasized the riskiness of the undertaking. Then, at night, the caravan would set out with little fanfare, making every effort to avoid tipping off brigands who might lie in wait in the surrounding countryside. Each member of the party kept his farewells brief. According to the Spanish chronicler Bernardino de Sahagún: "None entered the women's quarters, neither did any turn back or look to one side. If perchance he had gone forgetting something, he might no more come to take it, nor might they still go to offer it to him." Those who were left behind could only wait, worry, and, no doubt, dream of the riches that their loved ones might bring back.

Those riches were among the most prized in any Aztec market: translucent green jade, jaguar skins, and tortoise shells, seashells from the coast and gorgeous plumage from exotic tropical birds. Upon their return, however, the pochteca made no great show of their success. Arriving as they had left, under cover of darkness, they would hurriedly stow all their goods away from prying eyes before daylight. If a trader was caught on the street before he had hidden away his share, he would insist that the merchandise was not his but belonged to another merchant whom he was helping. At all times, they walked about with their eyes lowered in a gesture of humility and, except on special occasions, dressed in old clothing. All this was intended to avoid any appearance of challenging the governmental authorities or aspiring beyond their station.

The pochteca were happy with their lot in life, content to see their wealth and concurrent influence over economic affairs grow unobtrusively. Their word was already law in the marketplace, and they had little concern about how things functioned elsewhere. Had the conquest never occurred, they might one day have aspired to political power. But for the moment, they were more than satisfied to grow steadily richer and pass on their affluence to their heirs.

When the Spaniards arrived, the Aztec social structure stood intact. Class distinctions defined the very fabric of the culture, and no one had a clearer understanding of their significance than Motecuhzoma II. More than earlier rulers, he set himself above not only the common people but also the nobility. Even important members of the court were required to prostrate themselves before him, and noblemen carried his travel litter. Bernal Díaz noted the extreme deference shown to Motecuhzoma by the captains of the royal bodyguard, lauded personages in their own right: "They were obliged to take off their rich cloaks and put on others of little value. They had to be clean and to enter barefoot, with their eyes downcast, for they were not allowed to look him in the face. And they had to make him three obeisances, saying as they came toward him, 'Lord, my Lord, my great Lord!' Then when they had made their report, he would dismiss them with a few words. They did not turn their backs as they went out, but kept their faces toward him and their eyes to the ground, turning round only when they had left the room."

Traditionally, the various city-states of the central valley had elected their leaders, and the Aztecs had continued the practice, carrying it up to the highest levels of governance. In earlier times, the ruler was elected from a single family by heads of all the families in the community; later, as the upper classes emerged, the system evolved so that the ruler came to be chosen from the ranks of the royal family by a council of nobles, priests, and warriors.

Motecuhzoma apparently took matters even further. He was said to have dismissed all the officials of his predecessor's court chiefly on the grounds that they were of inferior descent. He supposedly allowed in his court only nobles of legitimate birth, rejecting those born of the exalted concubines traditionally permitted the elite.

In all things, he insisted on a rigid hierarchy, but this was hardly foreign to the Aztecs, who seemed to thrive on bureaucracy. Directly under the king was an official called the *cihuacoatl,* or woman-serpent, a strange title that was also the name of a goddess and probably derived from the fact that the position was originally occupied by the goddess's chief priest. In any event, the cihuacoatl was a kind of prime minister who handled the day-to-day running of the state, organizing military campaigns, handling royal finances, and serving as the nation's chief justice. Below him were four military commanders, corresponding to the four wards into which Tenochtitlan was divided by its main arteries. These five served as the ruler's closest advisers. The city's ruling council—a body of some hundred men in Motecuhzoma II's day—came next in line. A further sign of the times was that these officials, once elected by the various clans that had come together to form the Aztec nation, were by the late 15th century almost exclusively appointed by the ruler.

In addition to warriors and priests, there were a host of others in civil positions below these loftiest circles that also qualified as belonging to the ruling class, from taxgatherers and judges to clerks, messengers, and constables. "There were even officials in charge of sweeping," noted Durán. But the basic unit of political organization was more directly linked to the way the common people lived. Tenochtitlan was divided into dozens of small districts called *calpulli*, literally "great houses," each of which was headed by an elected chief, the *calpullec*. A particular calpulli could trace its origin to one of the ancestral groups, but by the 16th century, they were essentially residential associations that included parcels of communally owned farmland. A council made up of the heads of the calpulli's various families and chaired by the calpullec determined how the land should be allotted to meet each household's needs. In the days when he was the chief of a tightly knit clan, the calpullec had been a powerful figure; latterly, however, he had become a minor bureaucrat, much of his authority abrogated by the city council.

The people of the calpulli and two lower classes—the tenant farmers and the slaves—were the true lifeblood of the nation: They farmed its land, provided labor for the building of its temples, palaces, and causeways, and fashioned everything from its fabrics to its most exquisite artworks. The community at large was especially

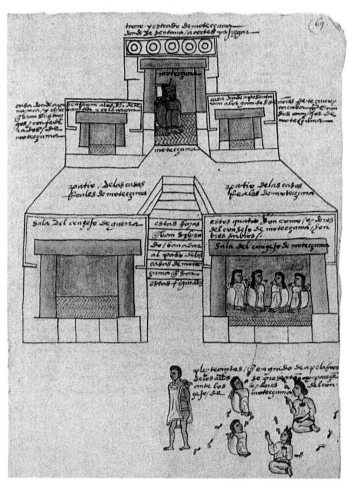

The terraced palace of Motecuhzoma II housed the ruler and his personal entourage upstairs, his counselors and guard below, as depicted in the Codex Mendoza. In its entirety, the complex boasted proportions far grander than the drawing suggests, and in fact almost amounted to a town in its own right.

The prominent features of a carved stone mask are rendered with a realism common to other Aztec masks but not typical of Aztec art in general, which was highly stylized. How such a piece—too heavy to wear—was used, no one can say.

enamored of its artisans and craftsmen. The people called them the *tolteca,* after the ethnic group that had spread through the valley before the Aztec ascendancy and were revered by the Aztecs for what they believed was their artistic achievement. The tolteca tended to congregate in certain wards and for the most part to associate only with the pochteca, who sold them feathers, gems, and gold, and who bought their fine jewelry, decorated shields, masks, and other treasured objects.

The Aztec attitude toward art, recorded in some of the texts produced after the Spanish conquest, put a premium on realism and clarity as a way of conveying religious and ceremonial concepts. Art was also considered to have value, this in a society that had yet to develop a monetary economy. Sahagún captured the popular sentiment: "Whatever the artist makes is an image of reality; he seeks its true appearance. If he makes a turtle, the carbon is fashioned thus: its shell as if it were moving, its head thrust out, seeming to move, its neck and feet as if it were stretching them out." Some artisans were said to be so skilled that they could cast a bird with a movable tongue or a fish with all its scales.

Naturally enough, the craftsman's best efforts were reserved for ceremonial items, and some of these precious objects have survived. During the excavation of the Great Temple in the early 1980s, archaeologists unearthed delicate jade and greenstone figurines, no doubt intended as offerings to various gods. Craftsmen produced intricately decorated vessels to hold *octli,* or pulque, an alcoholic drink fermented from the juice of the maguey plant that was consumed during certain rituals.

Many other forms of labor occupied the lives of average citizens. The women of practically every house spent their days spinning, weaving, and grinding corn. The men worked as potters or tanners, carpenters, builders, and quarrymen, as well as part-time farmers. Despite the rigorous insistence on class divisions, members of this vast middle class could, through their own efforts, be elevated to a higher station, either by distinguishing themselves in military service, by entering the priesthood, or perhaps by performing some special service for a member of the nobility.

At the bottom of society were the slaves. The Mesoamerican system of slavery was entirely different from the brutal practices of the invading Spaniards, who branded the faces of their captives with hot irons and forced them into killing labor in the mines. Only a few of the Aztec slaves were captives. Most came from the ranks of the Aztecs themselves, constituting a group known as the *tlacotin,* and they lived remarkably ordinary lives. They had become slaves for one of two reasons: They had been convicted of a crime and sentenced to pay for it through servitude, or they had voluntarily sold themselves into service. Aztec enslavement thus had, in a sense, moral underpinnings.

The vast majority were voluntary slaves, people who had fallen into poverty through la-

This intricate 15th-century crystal carving of a human skull, only four inches tall, represents in miniature a popular theme of Aztec art—death.

silver mask above, using the lost-wax method. This involved first covering a clay model of the object with beeswax, then plastering charcoal paste on top to make a mold. After the mold hardened, the artisan heated it until the wax dripped out, then poured molten metal in its place. Once the metal cooled, he broke away the mold.

Although fine pieces of Aztec metalwork existed in abundance 500 years ago, very few survive. In their lust for gold, the Spaniards melted works of art into bullion and shipped it home.

ziness or bad luck. Not surprisingly, a ceremony attended an individual's decision to give up his liberty; it helped ensure that he was treated fairly. Four respected witnesses were called together, and the prospective slave received his price, typically a load of mantles. He was allowed to remain free until he had gone through the payment, which might take a year or more. Then he reported to the man who had bought him—perhaps a merchant seeking porters, or a nobleman requiring farm labor or a household servant.

Except for the fact that he had to render service without pay, a slave retained the rights he had had as a free man. He could own goods and property and even buy slaves of his own, if he could somehow manage to acquire some collateral on the side. He could marry another slave or even a free woman; in either case, his children were born free. Some rose to positions of authority as overseers of estates or by marrying the widows of their masters. Women slaves often became their owners' concubines. One Aztec ruler, Itzcoatl, was the son of a slave woman.

Even bad slaves had certain protections. One who was dishonest or who failed to perform his duties had to be chastised three times in front of witnesses before his master could get rid of him. He was then put in a wooden collar and taken to the slave dealers' section of the market to be sold. Only after he had been thus sold off by three different masters did he suffer a harsher fate: He could then be purchased for sacrifice.

Regaining one's liberty was almost always a possibility. If a slave was resourceful enough to have saved up his original purchase price, he could buy back his freedom. Often a master would indicate that his slaves were to be released upon his death. Even the worst troublemakers were given a chance. In one of the more curious Aztec customs, a slave about to be sold at the market could legitimately make a dash for freedom. None but the master or the master's son could try to stop him, and anyone interfering with his attempted flight would be put into slavery himself. If the fugitive could make it to the royal palace—a distance of a little over a mile from the Tlatelolco market—he was declared free on the spot.

With the exception of a few types such as the incorrigible slaves, Aztecs across the entire social spectrum prized their dignity. They considered themselves inherently superior to the uncivilized nomads of the north. Good breeding and correct demeanor were of paramount importance, and bumptiousness was condemned. A civilized man was expected to walk quietly, eat carefully, revere his elders, and speak with gravity.

Sahagún gives perhaps the best depiction of this refined sensibility in his sketch of the Aztec physical ideal—a youth "slender like a reed; long and thin like a stout cane; well built; not of overfed body, not corpulent, and neither very small nor exceedingly tall." Women aimed at a related tastefulness and sense of moderation. They liked to lighten their bronze-brown skins to a pale yellow with a special ointment or cosmetic known as yellow earth, prepared from ocher. With the exception of the prostitutes, Tenochtitlan's women disdained the gaudy makeup and tattoos that were common in some other cities. One of the chronicles quotes a father admonishing his daughter on this issue: "Listen to me, child: Never make up your face nor paint it; never put red on your mouth to look beautiful. Makeup and paint are things that light women use—shameless creatures. If you want your husband to love you, dress well, wash yourself, and wash your clothes." Such descriptions suggest how stoical this great warrior people could be. The impression is confirmed by even a brief sampling of the many laws that helped maintain the social order—and the penalty, usually harsh in the extreme, imposed if they were broken.

Wearing clothes above one's station was considered a serious crime, sometimes punishable by death. According to a statute decreed by Motecuhzoma I in the mid-15th century and still in effect when the Spaniards arrived, only the nobility could wear cotton. "The common people will not be allowed to wear cotton clothing, under pain of death, but only garments of maguey fiber," said the ruler's law. A commoner's mantle could not be worn below the knees unless his legs had been scarred in battle. Furthermore, "No one but the great noblemen and chieftains is to build a house with a second story, under pain of death."

The list of crimes that could bring the death penalty was lengthy. Public drunkenness initially invoked the shaving of the drunk's head and the knocking down of his house; a second offense merited death. At least that was the rule for plebeians; members of the nobility never got a second chance.

CRIME AND PUNISHMENT

To enforce the upright, orderly conduct so valued by Aztec society, courts meted out stern sentences for offenses against the common good. Drunkenness—considered the root of most sin—earned the death penalty under certain circumstances, and anyone committing theft or adultery ran the risk of execution. The codices warn against every vice, portraying a loose-haired prostitute *(upper right)* and adulterers stoned to death for their infraction *(below, right)*.

Guilty persons who had not been caught could escape punishment by confessing to the goddess of filth, Tlazolteotl. Curiously, this deity—

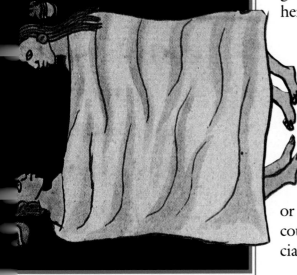

identified in Aztec art by a band of raw cotton on her headpiece and a dark spot around her nose and mouth *(below, left)*—not only absolved sin but also inspired it.

Scheduling a confession with the priests of Tlazolteotl required strategic timing, though, and people put it off as long as possible. The reason: They were allotted only one absolution in their lifetimes. Any subsequent crime could be punished to the full extent of the harsh Aztec law.

Again according to Motecuhzoma I's law, adulterers "are to be stoned and thrown in the rivers or to the buzzards." Judges could be put to death for taking a bribe, as could taxgatherers for embezzling. The message was unequivocal: No price was too high to maintain orderly conduct.

Irrespective of their class, then, most Aztecs shared a devotion to the social standards and codes of behavior of their culture. But more than this, they all tended to enjoy the same pleasures, revere the same mysteries, suffer the same weaknesses, and harbor the same fears. Noble and commoner alike took special joy in the birth of a child. As soon as a woman knew that she was pregnant, the whole local community began to get involved. Elders offered advice to the young parents and selected a midwife.

When her time had come, the mother-to-be took a sweat bath administered by the midwife and then was given an herbal beverage to help induce labor. If the drink had no effect, ground up opossum tail was provided. The Codex Borbonicus, the largest, most detailed, and most beautifully painted of the surviving codices, shows that she squatted to give birth, all the time attended by the midwife. After emitting the ritual battle cry indicating the mother's symbolic status as a warrior, the midwife cut the umbilical cord. A baby boy's cord was buried on a battlefield, in the hope that he might one day achieve great military fame; a girl's was buried beneath the hearth, signifying her dedication to the home.

Soon after the birth, the father sent for a diviner to determine the child's day sign—the most important indicator of the baby's future prospects. He consulted a special 260-day divinatory calendar (distinct from the regular 365-day solar calendar used for ritual purposes), which consisted of a combination of 13 numbers and 20 day names. Among the most propitious birthdates were 10 Eagle, which promised strength and courage, and 11 Vulture, which signaled a long and happy life. A boy unlucky enough to be born on 1 Jaguar, however, might end up a slave or a sacrificial victim. Fortunately, a better sign within a few days could offset such a negative reading, especially if the child was officially named on that day.

Four days of celebration followed the birth, during which

GODS, GODS, AND MORE GODS

The identity of this figure remains a mystery. He may be the fire, earth, or creator god.

Though primarily a corn goddess, Chicomecoatl wielded power over all sustenance in general and over fertility as well.

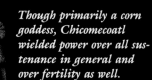

Bountiful harvests, military success, personal prosperity, the rising of the sun, and a whole lot more depended, the Aztecs believed, on the grace of their gods. As their society evolved their pantheon grew, until the Aztecs were worshiping such a bewildering variety of gods that keeping track of them could well have posed a difficult challenge for priests and populace alike. This proliferation of deities came about partly as a result of conquest, after which the local gods of vanquished peoples were taken over by the victors. Adding to the confusion, many deities overlapped in their functions;

for example, Chicomecoatl *(lower left)* was just one of a number of vegetation and fertility goddesses.

No day went by without the imputed needs and whims of the divinities being met, largely through rituals conducted at shrines and temples around the empire. Of the

Quetzalcoatl, here in a jade head-dress of quetzal plumes, created humankind and stood for knowledge.

hundreds of small, local temples that once existed throughout the land, the restored pyramid at Santa Cecilia Acatitlan *(opposite, below)*, near present-day Mexico City, gives an idea of what they looked like in their days of service. The destructive wrath of the Spaniards left none unsullied.

Snake-skirted Coatlicue, the mother of Huitzilopochtli, also gave birth to the moon and the stars.

time relatives came to visit, bringing presents and observing important rituals. As they entered the house, they rubbed ashes on their joints to protect the child from lameness or rheumatism. They also tended the fire, both to keep it from going out and to see that no one removed any burning logs from the house, "lest this action take renown from the child who had been born," as Sahagún put it.

Education, which was taken very seriously, began at the age of four, when children were given simple tasks and lessons: boys to fetch water, girls to learn the names and uses of household items. Later, in ordinary families, boys were taught to fish and handle boats. Girls learned to spin thread from maguey fiber and cotton, sweep, grind maize, and operate a loom.

A formal system of schools accommodated several different types of training and education. The *cuicacalli*, or houses of song, which were attached to temples, were meant for children both of the nobility and of the common classes. Boys and girls attended between ages 12 and 15, not only learning to sing and dance for ritual purposes but also picking up details of their people's history and religious beliefs. The songs they sang—often lasting well into the night—were filled with stories of creation, of life and death, of praise of the deities. Because singing and dancing were so important to a host of rituals and ceremonies, the youths were learning a vital part of their role in the community.

Another type of school associated with the temples was the *calmecac*, literally "row of houses." It was run by priests and priestesses primarily for the boys of noble families, although some chroniclers indicate that the children of traders and even plebeians were occasionally admitted. Students started at one of Tenochtitlan's several calmecacs anywhere between the ages of 10 and 15. They were taught the workings of the calendar and the interpretations of dreams and omens, and were required to memorize orations, songs, and histories. They learned glyphs, or pictographs, so that they might obtain guidance from the codices on the law, military arts, and other public concerns. The calmecac emphasized the art of self-expression and taught students how to speak well and to be respectful.

A boy who did not go to one of the calmecacs had to enroll at a *telpochcalli*, a "house of the young men." These schools were run by the elders and were primarily for commoners. Their chief purpose

143

An Aztec couple literally ties the knot in an illustration from the Codex Mendoza, linking their wedding garments in a traditional hearthside ceremony held at the groom's family home.

was to raise a new generation of warriors, but they too included in the curriculum history, religion, ritual, music, singing, dancing, and correct behavior. "Revere and greet your elders," ran one litany. "Console the poor and the afflicted with good works and words. Follow not the madmen who honor neither father nor mother; they are like animals, for they neither take nor hear advice. Do not mock the old, the sick, the maimed, or one who has sinned. Do not set a bad example, or speak indiscreetly, or interrupt the speech of another. If you are asked something, reply soberly and without affectation or flattery or prejudice to others. Wherever you go, walk with a peaceful air, and do not make wry faces or improper gestures."

In some ways, the calmecacs tended to be more severe in the treatment of their charges. Boys at both schools spent their days at hard work, much of it physical and disagreeable. But at the calmecac, a boy faced a kind of systematic degradation designed to toughen him. One father told his son who was about to enter a calmecac: "Listen, my son, you are not going to be honored, or obeyed, or esteemed. You are going to be looked down upon, humiliated, and despised. Every day you will cut maguey thorns for penance, and you will draw blood from your body with these spines, and you will bathe at night even when it is very cold. Harden your body to the cold, and when the time comes for fasting do not go and break your fast, but put a good face upon both fasting and penance."

The young men at the telpochcalli lived a quite different life. Certainly some of the deprivations were similar; according to one chronicler, "They ate but a little hard bread, and they slept with little

Showing wrinkles and other signs of age, this rendition of the old earth-goddess Toci, carved from basalt, realistically portrays an ordinary woman—seldom the subject of Aztec carvings.

covering and half exposed to the night air in rooms and quarters open like porches." But they also sang and danced and were permitted to consort with the young women known as *auianime,* a class of courtesans who attended to the sexual appetites of warriors. The student warriors spent little time at religious exercises. Sahagún condemned not only their free and easy relationship with women but also their manner of speaking. "They presumed to utter light and ironic words, and spoke with pride and temerity," he wrote. A predictable antagonism emerged between the young men of the calmecac and those of the telpochcalli, which found an outlet in mock battles, fought during the winter month of *Atemoztli.*

By age 20, a young man was permitted to marry; girls were betrothed earlier, at 14 or 15. The groom's relatives selected the bride with the aid of soothsayers who studied the prospective partners' birth signs to make sure the union would prosper. Matchmakers, usually old women, were hired to approach the bride's parents. Repeated visits were necessary to satisfy the requirements of good manners, and before the arrangements were made final, the girl's extended family was consulted.

At midday on the day of the wedding, the bride's parents gave an elaborate banquet—two or three days in preparation and supplied with luxury items to the full extent they could afford. The bride's face was adorned with yellow earth, her arms and legs bedecked with red feathers. When darkness fell, the wedding procession headed for the groom's home, with the bride carried piggyback by one of the matchmakers. The ceremony took place at the hearth and, among other things, involved tying the man's mantle to the woman's outer garment; from that moment they were officially married. Feasting resumed, and the older celebrants were allowed to get drunk on octli. The newlyweds eventually retired to the marriage chamber and stayed there in prayer for four days before they were permitted to consummate the marriage. On the fifth day they emerged, were cleansed, and then blessed by a priest. For the young man, this might be only the first of several marriages: A man in Aztec society could take several wives so long as he could support them.

Despite their concern to satisfy the rigorous and often somber demands of ritual, the Aztecs found plenty of opportunities to indulge their appetite for extravagance. In addition to the special occasions of births and weddings, the many holy days of the Aztec religious year were typically celebrated with grand displays of

Although a great deal of Aztec statuary depicts gods or nobles dressed in finery, this figure of andesite wears a loincloth like those shown in codex drawings of the common man.

feasting and dancing. Large segments of the population were drawn into the festivities. During the *hueytecuilhuitl*, the "great feast of the lords," singing and dancing began at sunset and went well into the night. Warriors and women cavorted between rows of torch holders, chanting all the while. Even the ruler sometimes came out and danced. This particular celebration lasted 10 days; it ended with the beheading and ritual sacrifice of a young woman adorned to represent the goddess of the young corn.

Even in their games, the Aztecs mixed orderliness and excess, seasoning their entertainment with a lusty dash of grim abandon. Their favorite sport was *ollamaliztli*, "the ball game." Only two Aztec ball courts have been excavated, but a description in the Florentine Codex has supplied many of the details of the rules of the game. The participants—almost always from the nobility—played with great enthusiasm. Injury was a constant danger; the hard rubber ball often bruised and occasionally killed. A relief panel from an earlier Mesoamerican period, unearthed in El Tajin on the Gulf Coast, shows the captain of a losing team stretched over a sacrificial stone and a victor plunging a knife into his chest. The Aztecs sometimes sacrificed prisoners of war on the ball courts, but apparently did not kill the losing captains, as had their predecessors. Nevertheless, the ball game was deeply imbued with religious and mythological meaning and with the imagery of death and sacrifice.

The ball game also appealed to another aspect of the national character. For all their austerity in other matters, the Aztecs were wild

Playing on I-shaped courts such as the one at Tenango southwest of Mexico City (top), noblemen could win the sometimes deadly game of ollamaliztli by driving a hard ball through a ring at center court, shown in the codex drawing above, or by scoring points at the opponents' goal. The game, which drew hordes of spectators, was a religious ritual as well as a sporting event, and was thought to signify the motions of the sun and the moon.

146

for gambling. Nobles and rich merchants wagered fortunes in expensive clothing and feathers on the ball games and on games of chance like *patolli,* a board game played with beans marked as dice. It was said that some men gambled all they had, including their houses. Some even sold themselves or their wives or children into slavery to satisfy the urge.

Something in the Aztecs' nature seemed always to veer toward the dark side of existence. "It is not true, it is not true," runs one of their poems, "that we come on this earth to live. We come only to sleep, only to dream. Our body is a flower. As grass becomes green in the springtime, so our hearts will open and give forth buds, and then they wither." Aztec lore is rich with instances of consultations with sorcerers, healings by magicians, spells and curses bought from wizards. Signs and portents lurked around every corner. Disaster was on the way if one saw a wolf crossing the road or a rabbit running into a house. The night was filled with monsters and headless creatures that pursued travelers. A person's birthday sign determined not only his earthly fate but also the time and circumstances of his death.

Most believed that powerful hallucinogenic plants—the peyote cactus or the *teonanacatl,* the "sacred mushroom"—would reveal with startling precision what the future held. Ingested during solemn rituals, they typically produced extraordinary visions. Sahagún described the result, which varied with the user: "Some saw that they were going to die, and wept; some saw themselves devoured by a wild beast; some saw themselves taking prisoners upon a battlefield, or else growing rich, or becoming the master of many slaves. Others saw that they would be convicted of adultery and that by reason of this crime their heads would be crushed."

A guilty conscience perhaps played a role in many of these hallucinations. Yet the Aztec religion, much like the Spaniards' own, seemed to provide an avenue for relief—with one major difference. An Aztec could confess his or her sins and wipe the slate clean, but only once. The prudent citizen thus tended to

Five Flower, the god of gambling, oversees four men playing patolli *in this codex illustration. The board game—which may have symbolized the Aztecs' 52-year calendar cycle—ruined many men.*

put off the unburdening as long as possible, sometimes waiting until death seemed imminent. Having decided it was time, the sinner consulted a soothsayer to determine the most auspicious day. Then, Sahagún was told, the sinner burned incense and listened to an exhortation by the priest before reciting his misdeeds in "the same order in which he committed them." The priest set a penance—perhaps fasting or drawing blood from the body or going naked except for a paper loincloth. The confessor was now ready to die.

For many, however, death itself, which lingered like a pall over so much of Aztec life, betrayed them yet again. Class divisions, it seemed, carried beyond the grave. Warriors could of course look forward to an Elysian bliss as hummingbirds and butterflies, and anyone who drowned was believed to go to the Southern Paradise, where Tlaloc reigned. The remaining masses went to Mictlan, the Land of the Dead, which was at best a region of all-consuming blackness. But getting there was hazardous. The journeyers had to cross eight layers of the underworld (Mictlan being the ninth and final layer), each full of peril, such as "the place of the obsidian-bladed winds." Belief held that the well-to-do could protect themselves by taking with them objects provided by their relatives, to be presented to the lord of the underworld. Some even had their servants killed and cremated so they could prepare food for them along the way. The poor, as always, had to take their chances, equipped for the journey with no more than a bowl of water and a few possessions. It was said that they suffered much on their way to the outer darkness. But in the end, when the Spaniards triumphed, no one—neither the powerful nor the weak—escaped the final death, the oblivion that overtook the great land of the Aztecs and left its amazing cities, monuments, and culture shattered, its people's spirit broken. Today, archaeologists and ethnohistorians patiently assemble the pieces, and once again the Aztecs live, this time in the imagination of the world.

INSIDE THE AZTEC WORLD

The might and grandeur of the Aztecs rested on the daily labors of unsung men and women who typically lived in modest mud-brick houses on small plots of swampland, where they fed, clothed, and educated their children. They farmed fields, wove cloth, hauled stones, dug canals, fired pots, shaped canoes, polished obsidian, hammered copper tools, and created objects of commanding beauty. On special occasions they went forth to carouse at festivals, bow to their rulers, and tremble in awe at religious rites.

Of their output, scant physical evidence remains. Textiles, featherwork, wooden implements, and foodstuffs perished long ago. Further, the Aztec custom of burning rather than burying their dead has left posterity with few of the items of furniture, clothing, and personal goods that often accompanied peoples of other cultures to the grave.

Yet, scholars have been able to piece together a de-tailed account of life in the Valley of Mexico five centuries ago. They have examined less perishable arti-facts—a handful of surviving murals and the more commonly found tools, weapons, pottery, and stone sculpture. Anthropologists also have observed contemporary peasants, many of whom live and work in much the same manner as their Aztec ancestors. The flower growers of Xochimilco, near Mexico City, for example, still farm small artificial islands in the swamp.

Finally, there is the evidence of vivid codex paintings, such as the depiction of a peasant *(above)* showing how he secured a burden on his back with a strap across his forehead. Such images, some of which appear on the following pages, have been carefully scrutinized, sometimes in ingenious ways. By studying the pictures in 24 codices and several murals, for example, one costume expert was able to determine the type of clothing pre-scribed for each Aztec class and occupation.

THE PLEASURES— AND SURPRISES—OF THE AZTEC TABLE

Motecuhzoma's cooks prepared as many as 30 different dishes for each dinner. The elite sat down in their homes to meals that, while not as sumptuous as those of their ruler, were nutritious and varied. Bernardino de Sahagún reported that an Aztec menu might include newts with yellow peppers, locusts with sage, or venison with chilies, tomatoes, and squash seeds.

Farmers raised turkeys for special occasions. Hunters sometimes provided duck, pheasant, deer, or wild boar, but more often brought home rabbits, crows, and pigeons. Lake Tetzcoco yielded frogs, fish, and assorted freshwater creatures.

Staples—corn, tomatoes, sweet potatoes, turkeys, and chilies—have since enriched menus worldwide. But other foods, including algae, corn smut, larvae nests, insect eggs, water flies and their nests, larvae, salamanders, iguanas, and armadillos, all of which were relished by the Aztecs, have not become international delicacies, although agave worms and ant eggs are still considered a treat in Mexico.

Mashed, boiled with cornmeal, and seasoned with honey, cacao beans (above) were blended into a frothy drink known as chocolatl. It was so valued that the beans served as currency.

Laying up a food supply, women fill vessels with dried corn kernels. This important staple could be stored for months on end without deterioration.

Seated on the ground for the day's main meal, a family enjoys its typical menu—tortillas and a prepared dish, probably beans with a chili or tomato sauce. At an earlier, lighter meal, they often ate a gruel made from amaranth (a grain) or corn. They fattened their hairless, non-barking itzcuintli dogs, a sculpted example of which is shown below, for feasts.

Decorated with paintings of plants and animals, this bowl is incised on the bottom in a criss-cross pattern. Chilies were grated against the protruding segments.

151

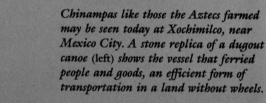

Chinampas like those the Aztecs farmed may be seen today at Xochimilco, near Mexico City. A stone replica of a dugout canoe (left) shows the vessel that ferried people and goods, an efficient form of transportation in a land without wheels.

A young woman weaves on a back-strap loom attached to a pole, with the other end strapped around her back. Leaning backward, she could vary the tension on the warp. A rod lifted every other warp thread so the shuttle could be passed through the weft in one quick movement.

THE MANY REWARDS AND BENEFITS OF HARD LABOR

Each day the Aztec worker rose to begin hours of toil in communal fields, on public projects, or on officially controlled crafts. His wife, in turn, devoted much of her day to weaving, pausing from time to time to look after the children or livestock and to barter in the market and cook family meals.

A growing need for farmland forced the use of shallow, marshy areas of the lake. A grid of channels was dug, and the extremely fertile lake-bottom soil was piled onto each rectangle, or *chinampa*. This resulted in a checkerboard of narrow strips of land about 300 feet long and 15 to 30 feet wide, surrounded by canals. Farmers could live on these island plots and grow flowers and vegetables, watering their crops with buckets toted from the adjoining canal.

In production all year round, with fresh mud dredged up when necessary, chinampas yielded several crops annually. Extracting produce from every foot of available earth led to a food surplus, freeing some workers to specialize in crafts or to labor at public works.

Using a pointed wooden stick to loosen the soil, a farmer drops seeds into the holes he has made in the top of each mound. He carries his seed corn in the cloth tied over his shoulder.

Kernels of corn were ground between stone manos and metates like this set found at Teotihuacan, similar to ones used today by Mexican peasants. The resulting cornmeal was shaped into cakes baked on a clay griddle.

DRUMMING A LIVELY BEAT AT FESTIVE RITES AND FEASTS

Religious festivals throbbed with vigorous rhythms, since music enlivened both solemn rituals and joyful feasts. Professional singers and dancers performed at every sacred ceremony, accompanied by small orchestras playing flutes, whistles, shell trumpets, gourd-and-stick rattles, gongs, and drums. Dancers added to the percussive effect by attaching strands of shells, bones, or copper bells to their clothing so they would jingle as they moved.

Following the ceremonies, many festivalgoers sat down to sumptuous banquets in the homes of the wealthy, where they enjoyed music, poetry recitations, and plays performed by professional entertainers attached to the noble households. Poetry was recited to the beat of drums and the melody of flutes. The guests often joined in chanting and singing. Some rose to fling themselves into the dance, as the clay figure of a dancer at a festival *(right)*, wearing lip and ear plugs, appears to have done.

At Motecuhzoma's feasts, however, a sad fate might await the vocalist who sang off-key, or the drummer who missed a beat. "They imprisoned him and he died," noted the chronicler Sahagún.

The finger holes of the Aztec flute above suggest that a pentatonic, or five-note, scale might have been in use. Double and triple flutes, however, have been found with as many as 16 stops.

154

Warriors dressed as eagles and
jaguars dance to the pulsing
rhythm of the teponaztli, a two-
toned wooden gong beaten with
rubber-tipped sticks, and the hue-
huetl, a drum hollowed from a log.

The charming ceramic turtle above is an
ocarina. Its tail forms the mouthpiece,
with the sound issuing from the mouth.

155

FULFILLING THE DEMAND FOR BEAUTY AND STYLE

Rulers and nobles of the Valley of Mexico competed for the skills of the finest artisans, who worked in more than 30 officially recognized crafts. Guilds set standards for payment and quality by ranking their members. The craftsmen lived in their own section of Tenochtitlan, to which they flocked from villages throughout the empire.

Metalworkers hammered gold and silver into jewelry and religious artifacts and fashioned copper into needles, fishhooks, drill heads, chisels, and axes. Stonecutters used copper tools, together with water and abrasive sand, to cut, drill, and polish turquoise, obsidian, jade, amethyst, carnelian, and alabaster into jewelry and sacred objects. Most prestigious of all were the featherworkers, who plucked the brilliant plumage of green quetzals, scarlet macaws, blue cotingas, and parrots to create colorful headdresses, shields, tunics, and mantles.

The rabbit-shaped calcite drinking cup above was produced with copper tools, then polished. Rabbits symbolized drunken revelry, and the cup might have held octli, an alcoholic beverage made from maguey sap. Only old people could get drunk without punishment, which included beating to death and strangling.

A warrior's pendant in the shape of an animal head (right) is a mosaic of turquoise with a garnet mouth displaying fish teeth. Considered second only to jade as the most precious of gemstones, turquoise symbolized water and sky.

At the center of a fan of feathers and bamboo (above) rests a stylized butterfly; a floral design decorates the reverse side. Using a bone spatula, an artisan would glue feathers to a sheet of cotton (right). The fabric had earlier been backed with maguey leaves, stiffened with a dried coat of glue, and stenciled with a design.

A CHAIN OF CULTURES IN THE NEW WORLD

In the Valley of Mexico, a natural basin a mile and a half high in the heart of Mesoamerica, hunting and fishing communities appeared as early as 20,000 BC. By 5000 BC, on the shores of Lake Tetzcoco, seminomadic hunters had begun farming corn, weaving baskets, and molding pottery. By 1500 BC, farmers were building mud-hut villages. Civilization accelerated, and in another 300 years Olmec culture, emerging in the lowlands to the southeast, had spread to the valley. The Olmecs were the first of a string of regional civilizations, described on the right. Lacking wheeled vehicles or beasts of burden, successive groups of settlers gradually created a Mesoamerican lifestyle that culminated in the artistic and societal grandeur of the Aztecs.

EARLY & MIDDLE PRECLASSIC: 1200-400 BC

OLMEC HEAD

The Olmecs developed hieroglyphs and a calendar, and created networks of communication and trade that linked population centers throughout Mesoamerica. The region's first great civilization left its imprint most dramatically in sculptures of giant heads (*above*) carved from basalt. About nine feet high and weighing as much as 40 tons, they are thought to be portraits of Olmec rulers. The stones used were probably quarried in the mountains near Tuxtla, 80 miles from their ultimate destination. Dragged to the rivers, they were floated on rafts to the city to be carved. This complex enterprise could not have been achieved without clearly defined social classes.

Other statues were of Olmec gods and combined features of humans and jaguars, crocodiles, and other formidable creatures. The Olmec system of religious and societal leadership would persist through all succeeding Mesoamerican cultures.

LATE PRECLASSIC: 400 BC-AD 100

"PRETTY LADY"

Situated on the outskirts of Olmec culture, the people of the Valley of Mexico lived in small villages where they grew corn and made attractive pottery figures like the so-called Pretty Lady, from the Tlatilco village clay pits (*above*). At the southern edge of the valley, a settlement at Cuicuilco developed as a cultural center about 400 BC, eventually acquiring a population of more than ten thousand. At its ceremonial hub stood a temple—a tiered circular mound of earth some 390 feet long, faced with stones, rising in four steps to a center 75 feet high.

Toward the end of this period, the city of Teotihuacan, in the northeast section of the valley, began to compete with Cuicuilco for regional influence. Around 200 BC, Cuicuilco was destroyed by the first of two volcanic eruptions, leaving Teotihuacan unchallenged.

CLASSIC: AD 100-750

FEATHERED SERPENT

By AD 100, Teotihuacan dominated the Valley of Mexico, spreading its influence throughout Mesoamerica. Occupying eight square miles, it had a population that may have increased to 200,000 by AD 500 and ranked as one of the largest cities of its era in the world. At its heart lay a spectacular complex of massive pyramids, which remain today as one of the hemisphere's splendors. One of these may have been dedicated to Quetzalcoatl, meaning "feathered serpent" (*above*), a fertility deity. The city's art resonated with military themes. Surrounding the sacred center stood palaces containing beautiful murals, as well as large multifamily apartment compounds.

Located near obsidian deposits, Teotihuacan developed and controlled an important obsidian industry. Raw stone was brought into the city to be crafted into products traded throughout Mesoamerica. Artisans also introduced cylindrical pottery that stood on three legs. Teotihuacan's influence ended circa AD 750, when much of the city was burned.

EPICLASSIC: AD 750-900	EARLY POSTCLASSIC: AD 900-1250	LATE POSTCLASSIC: AD 1250-1521	EARLY COLONIAL PERIOD: AD 1521

EPICLASSIC: AD 750-900

JAGUAR KNIGHT

EARLY POSTCLASSIC: AD 900-1250

TOLTEC WARRIOR

LATE POSTCLASSIC: AD 1250-1521

AZTEC EAGLE

EARLY COLONIAL PERIOD: AD 1521

SPANISH HELMET

The fall of Teotihuacan marked the end of centuries of trade and the decline of the high level of culture that had developed in and around the Valley of Mexico, ushering in a new era of frequent warfare. As a power vacuum developed, lesser groups from far-flung parts of Mesoamerica began to establish themselves in the region. Their villages grew into defendable cities that competed with each other for economic and military power. No single city held sway; instead, a number of regional centers evolved, such as Cacaxtla, whose buildings were painted with scenes of warfare, as is shown in the mural fragment above.

Among the new towns was Tula, about 40 miles northwest of Teotihuacan. Its inhabitants, a mix of peoples who had lived in the area for centuries and new settlers whose forebears had been seminomads, became known as the Toltecs. By about AD 1000, Tula numbered perhaps 40,000, with an equal population in the outlying farmlands. Tula's ceremonial center was small, surrounded by well-built housing. Upon a five-step pyramidal platform stood a row of 15-foot-tall stone columns carved as warriors *(above)*. Religious objects emphasized human sacrifice. Racks were erected to display captives' skulls, and temples contained *chacmools,* stone altars for sacrificed human hearts.

The Toltecs established a tribute-exacting empire dominating much of central Mexico, and their influence spread to the southern lowlands. Their imperial system became a model for the later Aztecs. Although built on a defensible hilltop, Tula, too, collapsed and fell into ruin around AD 1200.

Relative latecomers, the Aztecs, seminomadic Chichimecs from the northwest, arrived in the Valley of Mexico about AD 1200. They brought along a representation of their fearsome tribal god, Huitzilopochtli, whom they placated with human sacrifice. According to legend, he had told them to settle where an eagle perched on a cactus *(above)*. The bird was allegedly seen in the marshlands of an island in Lake Tetzcoco about AD 1325. There the Aztecs built their canal-laced city, Tenochtitlan.

At the center of Tenochtitlan, the Aztecs erected a spacious religious precinct of stunning pyramids and temples. They farmed *chinampas,* small fertile islands dredged from the swamp. Aggressive warriors, they demanded tribute from the city-states within their growing empire. The city's wealth, commerce, and culture attracted settlers, and by 1519 Tenochtitlan housed perhaps as many as 200,000 people, approximately three times the population of Spain's largest city, Seville.

In 1521, the Valley of Mexico was conquered by Spaniards, their iron helmets *(above)* gleaming in startling contrast to the colorful feathers of their adversaries. Unlike earlier invaders, they had no desire to absorb the ways of the conquered peoples; instead, they were determined to force the Aztecs to adopt the values and religion of Spain. Deliberately and thoroughly, the civil administration, abetted by the Catholic Church, tried to obliterate every vestige of the literature, religion, and traditions of the new land. Within a decade after the conquest, churchmen, still combating Aztec influences, found it necessary to reconstruct in writing the civilization they were trying so hard to crush, if only to better understand it. Ultimately, Aztec ways, gradually seeping into the newly planted culture, created not a Spanish replica but a vigorous hybrid.

ACKNOWLEDGMENTS

The editors wish to thank the following for their valuable assistance in the preparation of this volume:

Donatella Bertoni, IGDA, Milan; Elizabeth Boone, Dumbarton Oaks Libraries, Washington, D.C.; Michael Coe, Peabody Museum of Natural History, Yale University, New Haven, Connecticut; W. M. Ferguson, Wellington, Kansas; Peter Furst, Devon, Pennsylvania; David Grove, University of Illinois, Urbana; Sabine Hesse, Württembergisches Landesmuseum, Stuttgart; Caterina Longanesi, Milan; Eduardo Matos Moctezuma, Dirección General de Templo Mayor, Mexico City; Donato Pineider, Florence, Italy; Michael Spence, Department of Anthropology, Social Science Centre, Ontario, Canada; Richard Townsend, Art Institute of Chicago, Chicago, Illinois.

PICTURE CREDITS

Anthropology and History, Mexico. 101: Nick Saunders, London/National Institute of Anthropology and History, Mexico; background Eberhard Thiem, Lotos Film, Kaufbeuren. 102: Michel Zabé/National Institute of Anthropology and History, Mexico. 104, 105: Salvador Guilliem—from the catalogue *Art of Aztec Mexico: Treasures of Tenochtitlan,* National Gallery of Art, Washington, D.C./National Institute of Anthropology and History, Mexico. 106: Miguel Salgado from "The National Museum of Anthropology, Mexico," ©Pedro Ramirez Vazquez, 1968, Panorama Editorial, Mexico. 107: Copied by Donato Pineider, Florence/Biblioteca Medicea Laurenziana, Florence. 109: Museo de America, Madrid. 110, 111: Mark Godfrey/D. Brown & Assoc.; art by Fred Holz. 112: Art by Fred Holz—Michel Zabé/National Institute of Anthropology and History, Mexico. 113: Kenneth Garrett/National Institute of Anthropology and History, Mexico (2). 114: Art by Fred Holz—Enrique Franco Torrijos/National Institute of Anthropology and History, Mexico; Salvador Guilliem/National Institute of Anthropology and History, Mexico. 115-117: Kenneth Garrett/National Institute of Anthropology and History, Mexico. 118: Michel Zabé/National Institute of Anthropology and History, Mexico (3). 119: Mario Carrieri, Milan/National Institute of Anthropology and History, Mexico; Michel Zabé/National Institute of Anthropology and History, Mexico. 120: Michel Zabé/National Institute of An-

thropology and History, Mexico. 121: Art by Fred Holz; Michel Zabé/National Institute of Anthropology and History, Mexico—Salvador Guilliem/National Institute of Anthropology and History, Mexico. 122-123: Art by Fred Holz—Michel Zabé/National Institute of Anthropology and History, Mexico (3). 124: René Percheron/Artephot/National Institute of Anthropology and History, Mexico. 126, 127: Bob Schalkwijk/National Institute of Fine Arts, Mexico. 128: Eberhard Thiem, Lotos Film, Kaufbeuren. 131: Bibliothèque Nationale, Paris. 132: National Institute of Anthropology and History, Mexico—Debra Nagao/National Institute of Anthropology and History, Mexico. 133: Richard Townsend, Art Institute of Chicago—art by Time-Life Books. 136: Bodleian Library, Oxford. 137: Werner Forman Archive/Museum für Völkerkunde, Hamburg. 138: Werner Forman Archive, London—photographed by J. Oster/Musée de l'Homme, Paris. 139: Salvador Guilliem/National Institute of Anthropology and History, Mexico—photo by Peter T. Furst. 140: Bibliothèque de l'Assemblée Nationale, Paris. 141: Copied by Donato Pineider, Florence/Biblioteca Medicea Laurenziana, Florence—Bodleian Library, Oxford. 142: Werner Forman Archive/Museum für Völkerkunde, Basel—Foto Dietrich Graf/Museum für Völkerkunde SMPK, Berlin; Werner Forman Archive, London; Werner Forman Archive/British Museum, London. 143: René

Percheron/Artephot/National Institute of Anthropology and History, Mexico. 144: Bodleian Library, Oxford—photo by Peter T. Furst. 145: Photo by Peter T. Furst/National Institute of Anthropology and History, Mexico. 146, 147: John Carlson, Center for Archaeoastronomy—G. Dagli Orti, Paris—Scala, Florence/Biblioteca Nazionale Centrale, Florence. 149: Bodleian Library, Oxford. 150: Michel Zabé—copied by Donato Pineider, Florence/Biblioteca Medicea Laurenziana, Florence. 151: Copied by Donato Pineider, Florence/Biblioteca Medicea Laurenziana, Florence; photo by Peter T. Furst—Foto Dietrich Graf/Museum für Völkerkunde SMPK, Berlin. 152: Werner Forman Archive, London—Salvador Guilliem/National Institute of Anthropology and History, Mexico—Bodleian Library, Oxford. 153: Copied by Donato Pineider, Florence/Biblioteca Medicea Laurenziana, Florence—Eberhard Thiem, Lotos Film, Kaufbeuren. 154: Eberhard Thiem, Lotos Film, Kaufbeuren; Werner Forman Archive/Museum für Völkerkunde, Berlin. 155: G. Dagli Orti, Paris—Werner Forman Archive, London/British Museum. 156: Werner Forman Archive/National Institute of Anthropology and History, Mexico—British Museum, London. 157: Eberhard Thiem, Lotos Film, Museum für Völkerkunde, Vienna; copied by Donato Pineider, Florence/Biblioteca Medicea Laurenziana, Florence. 158, 159: Art by Paul Breeden. End paper: Art by Paul Breeden.

BIBLIOGRAPHY

BOOKS

Anderson, Arthur J. O., and Charles E. Dibble (Trans.). *The War of Conquest.* Salt Lake City: University of Utah Press, 1978.

Aveni, Anthony F., and Gary Urton (Eds.). *Ethnoastronomy and Archaeoastronomy in the American Trop-* ics. New York: New York Academy of Sciences, 1982.

Baquedano, Elizabeth. *Aztec Sculpture.* London: British Museum Publications, 1984.

Batres, Leopoldo. *Teotihuacan: La Ciudad Sagrada de los Toltecas.* Mexico City: Talleres de la Escuela N. de Artes & Oficios, 1889.

Berdan, Frances F.:
The Aztecs. New York: Chelsea House Publishers, 1989. *The Aztecs of Central Mexico: An Imperial Society.* New York: Holt, Rinehart and Winston, 1982.

Bernal, Ignacio:

A History of Mexican Archaeology: The Vanished Civilizations of Middle America. London: Thames and Hudson, 1980.
Mexico before Cortez: Art, History, Legend (rev. ed.). Translated by Willis Barnstone. Garden City: Anchor Press, 1975.

Berrelleza, Juan Alberto Romá. *Sacrificio de Niños en el Templo Mayor*. Mexico City: Instituto Nacional de Antropología e Historia, 1990.

Berrin, Kathleen (Ed.). *Feathered Serpents and Flowering Trees*. San Francisco: Fine Arts Museums of San Francisco, 1988.

Boone, Elizabeth Hill (Ed.):
The Art and Iconography of Late Post-Classic Central Mexico. Washington, D.C.: Dumbarton Oaks, 1982.
The Aztec Templo Mayor. Washington, D.C.: Dumbarton Oaks, 1983.
Ritual Human Sacrifice in Mesoamerica. Washington, D.C.: Dumbarton Oaks, 1984.

Bray, Warwick. *Everyday Life of the Aztecs*. New York: Dorset Press, 1968.

Brizuela, María Luisa Franco. *Conservación del Templo Mayor de Tenochtitlan*. Mexico City: Instituto Nacional de Antropología e Historia, 1990.

Broda, Johanna, Davíd Carrasco, and Eduardo Matos Moctezuma. *The Great Temple of Tenochtitlan: Center and Periphery in the Aztec World*. Berkeley: University of California Press, 1987.

Burland, Cottie, and Werner Forman. *Gods and Fate in Ancient Mexico*. London: Orbis Publishing, 1980.

Carrasco, Davíd:
Quetzalcoatl and the Irony of Empire: Myths and Prophecies in the Aztec Tradition. Chicago: University of Chicago Press, 1982.
Religions of Mesoamerica. San Francisco: Harper & Row, 1990.

Carrasco, Davíd (Ed.). *To Change Place: Aztec Ceremonial Landscapes*. Niwot: University Press of Colorado, 1991.

Ceram, C. W. *Gods, Graves, and Scholars*. New York: Alfred A. Knopf, 1972.

Charnay, Désiré. *The Ancient Cities of the New World: Being Voyages and Explorations in Mexico and Central America from 1857-1882*. Translated by J. Gonino and Helen S. Conant. New York: AMS Press, 1973.

Codex Mendoza: Aztec Manuscript. Fribourg: Productions Liber, 1978.

Coe, Michael D.:
America's First Civilization. New York: American Heritage Publishing, 1968.
Mexico (2d ed.). London: Thames and Hudson, 1977.
Mexico (3d ed.). London: Thames and Hudson, 1984.

Coe, Michael D., Dean Snow, and Elizabeth Benson. *Atlas of Ancient America*. New York: Facts On File Publications, 1986.

Davies, Nigel:
The Ancient Kingdoms of Mexico. New York: Penguin Books, 1983.
The Aztecs: A History. New York: G. P. Putnam's, 1974.

Díaz, Bernal. *The Conquest of New Spain*. Nashville: Fisk University Press, 1932.

Dickey, Thomas, Vance Muse, and Henry Wiencek. *The God-Kings of Mexico*. New York: Stonehenge Press, 1982.

Diehl, Richard A. *Tula: The Toltec Capital of Ancient Mexico*. London: Thames and Hudson, 1983.

D'Olwer, Luis Nicolau. *Fray Bernardino de Sahagún*. Salt Lake City: University of Utah Press, 1987.

Durán, Diego:
Aztecs: The History of the Indies of New Spain. Translated by Doris Heyden and Fernando Horcasitas. New York: Orion Press, 1964.
Book of the Gods and Rites and the Ancient Calendar. Edited and translated by Fernando Horcasitas and Doris Heyden. Norman: University of Oklahoma Press, 1971.

Edmonson, Munro S. (Ed.). *Sixteenth Century Mexico: The Work of Sahagún*. Albuquerque: University of New Mexico Press, 1974.

Ekholm, Gordon F., and Ignacio Bernal. *Archaeology of Northern Mesoamerica* (Part 1). Austin: University of Texas Press, 1971.

Fagan, Brian M.:
The Aztecs. New York: W. H. Freeman, 1984.
Quest for the Past. Addison-Wesley, 1978.

Ferguson, William M., and Arthur H. Rohn. *Mesoamerica's Ancient Cities*. Niwot: University Press of Colorado, 1990.

Furst, Jill Leslie, and Peter T. Furst. *Pre-Columbian Art of Mexico*. New York: Abbeville Press, 1980.

Gillmor, Frances. *Flute of the Smoking Mirror*. Albuquerque: University of New Mexico Press, 1949.

Grove, David. *Chalcatzingo: Excavations on the Olmec Frontier*. London: Thames and Hudson, 1984.

Hagen, Victor Wolfgang von. *The Aztec Man and Tribe*. New York: New American Library, 1961.

Hassig, Ross:
Aztec Warfare: Imperial Expansion and Political Control. Norman: University of Oklahoma Press, 1988.
Trade, Tribute, and Transportation. Norman: University of Oklahoma Press, 1985.

Heyden, Doris, and Luis Francisco Villaseñor. *The Great Temple and the Aztec Gods*. Mexico City: Minutiae Mexicana, 1984.

Holmes, William H. *Archeological Studies among the Ancient Cities of Mexico*. Chicago: Field Columbian Museum, 1897.

Innes, Hammond. *The Conquistadors*. New York: Alfred A. Knopf, 1969.

Kandell, Jonathan. *La Capital: The Biography of Mexico City*. New York: Random House, 1988.

Leonard, Jonathan Norton, and the Editors of Time-Life Books. *Ancient America* (Great Ages of Man series). Alexandria, Va.: Time-Life Books, 1979.

McIntosh, Jane. *The Practical Archaeologist*. New York: Facts On File Publications, 1986.

Matos Moctezuma, Eduardo:
The Aztecs. New York: Rizzoli International Publications, 1989.
The Great Temple of the Aztecs: Treasures of Tenochtitlan. London:Thames and Hudson, 1988.
Official Guide: The Great Temple. Mexico City: INAH-Salvat, 1990.
Teotihuacán: The City of Gods. New York: Rizzoli International Publications, 1990.

Treasures of the Great Temple. La Jolla, Calif.: Alti Publishing, 1990.

Meyer, Karl E.:
The Pleasures of Archaeology: A Visa to Yesteryear. New York: Atheneum, 1971.
Teotihuacán. New York: Newsweek, 1973.

Meyer, Michael C., and William L. Sherman. *The Course of Mexican History* (3d ed.). New York: Oxford University Press, 1987.

Millon, René. *The Teotihuacán Map* (Vol. 1 of *Urbanization at Teotihuacán, Mexico,* edited by René Millon). Austin: University of Texas Press, 1973.

National Museum of Anthropology, Mexico City (Great Museums of the World series). Milan: Newsweek & Arnoldo Mondadori Editore, 1970.

Nicholson, H. B. *Art of Aztec Mexico: Treasures of Tenochtitlan.* Washington, D.C.: National Gallery of Art, 1983.

Pagden, A. R. (Ed. and Trans.). *Hernan Cortes: Letters from Mexico.* New York: Grossman Publishers, 1971.

Parkes, Henry Bamford. *A History of Mexico.* Boston: Houghton Mifflin, 1970.

Pasztory, Esther. *Aztec Art.* New York: Harry N. Abrams, 1983.

Prescott, William H. *History of the Conquest of Mexico.* (3 vols.). Edited by John Foster Kirk. Philadelphia: J. B. Lippincott, 1873.

Reed, Alma M. *The Ancient Past of Mexico.* New York: Crown Publishers, 1966.

Sabloff, Jeremy A. *The Cities of Ancient Mexico.* New York: Thames and Hudson, 1990.

Sahagún, Bernardino de:
Florentine Codex: General History of the Things of New Spain (13 vols., 2d ed., rev.). Translated by Arthur J. O. Anderson and Charles E. Dibble. Salt Lake City: School of American Research, 1975.
A History of Ancient Mexico. Translated by Fanny R. Bandelier. Nashville: Fisk University Press, 1932.

Soustelle, Jacques. *Daily Life of the Aztecs.* Translated by Patrick O'Brian. Stanford, Calif.: Stanford University Press, 1970.

Spinden, Herbert J. *Ancient Civilizations of Mexico and Central America.* New York: American Museum of Natural History, 1922.

Splendors of Thirty Centuries. New York: Metropolitan Museum of Art, 1990.

Sten, María. *Codices of Mexico and Their Extraordinary History.* Translated by Carolyn B. Czitrom. Mexico City: Ediciones Lara, 1978.

Stierlin, Henri. *Living Architecture: Ancient Mexican.* New York: Grosset & Dunlap, 1968.

Stuart, Gene S. *The Mighty Aztecs.* Washington, D.C.: National Geographic Society, 1981.

Tompkins, Peter. *Mysteries of the Mexican Pyramids.* New York: Harper & Row, 1976.

Vaillant, George C. *Aztecs of Mexico.* Harmondsworth (U.K.): Penguin Books, n.d.

Vazquez, Pedro Ramirez. *The National Museum of Anthropology, Mexico.* Translated by Mary Jean Labadie and Aza Zatz. New York: Helvetica Press, 1968.

Weaver, Muriel Porter. *Aztecs, Maya, and Their Predecessors.* New York: Seminar Press, 1972.

Wicke, Charles R. *Olmec: An Early Art Style of Pre-Columbian Mexico.* Tucson: University of Arizona Press, 1971.

Wilson, Rex L. (Ed.). *Rescue Archeology: Proceedings of the Second New World Conference on Rescue Archeology.* Dallas: Southern Methodist University Press, 1987.

Wilson, Rex L., and Gloria Loyola (Eds.). *Rescue Archeology: Papers from the First New World Conference on Rescue Archeology.* Washington, D.C.: Preservation Press, 1982.

The World Atlas of Archaeology. Boston: G. K. Hall, 1985.

Yoffee, Norman, and George L. Cowgill (Eds.). *The Collapse of Ancient States and Civilizations.* Tucson: University of Arizona Press, 1988.

PERIODICALS

Anawalt, Patricia:
"Costume and Control: Aztec Sumptuary Laws." *Archaeology* (New York), January/February 1980.
"Understanding Aztec Human Sacrifice." *Archaeology* (New York), September/October 1982.
"What Price Aztec Pageantry?" *Archaeology* (New York), July 1977.

Austin, Alfredo López, Leonardo López Luján, and Saburo Sugiyama. "The Temple of Quetzalcoatl at Teotihuacan: Its Possible Ideological Significance." *Ancient Mesoamerica* (Cambridge), 1991, Vol. 2, pp. 93-105.

Castro, Rubén Cabrera, Saburo Sugiyama, and George L. Cowgill. "The Templo de Quetzalcoatl Project at Teotihuacan: A Preliminary Report." *Ancient Mesoamerica* (Cambridge), 1991, Vol. 2, pp. 77-92.

Chávez, Raul García, et al. "The INAH Salvage Archaeology Excavations at Azcapotzalco, Mexico." *Ancient Mesoamerica* (Cambridge), 1990, Vol. 1, pp. 225-232.

Clendinnen, Inga. "The Cost of Courage in Aztec Society." *Past & Present* (Oxford), May 1985.

Heyden, Doris. "An Interpretation of the Cave underneath the Pyramid of the Sun in Teotihuacan, Mexico." *American Antiquity* (Salt Lake City), April 1975.

McDowell, Bart. "The Aztecs." *National Geographic,* December 1980.

Manzanilla, Linda, and Luis Barba. "The Study of Activities in Classic Households." *Ancient Mesoamerica* (Cambridge), 1990, Vol. 1, pp. 41-49.

Matos Moctezuma, Eduardo:
"The Great Temple of Tenochtitlán." *Scientific American,* August 1984.
"New Finds in the Great Temple." *National Geographic,* December 1980.

Millon, René:
"Teotihuacán." *Scientific American,* June 1967.
"Teotihuacán: Completion of Map of Giant Ancient City in the Valley of Mexico." *Science,* December 1970.

Montellano, Bernard Ortiz de. "Empirical Aztec Medicine." *Science,* April 18, 1975.

Montes, Augusto F. Molina. "The Building of Tenochtitlan." *National Geographic,* December 1980.

Nuño, Rubén Bonifaz. "The Hall of the Eagle." *Artes de Mexico* (Mexico City), Spring 1990.

OTHER SOURCES

"In Situ Archaeological Conservation." Proceedings of Meetings of the Instituto Nacional de Antropología e Historia, Mexico, and the Getty Conservation Trust. Century City, Calif.: Getty Conservation Institute, 1986.

Parsons, Jeffrey R. "Prehistoric Settlement Patterns in the Texcoco Region, Mexico." Memoirs of the Museum of Anthropology, no. 3. Ann Arbor: University of Michigan, 1971.

MUSEUMS

Readers interested in viewing Aztec objects will find outstanding collections in the following institutions.

American Museum of Natural History, New York

Anahuacalli, Museo Diego Rivera, Mexico City

Brooklyn Museum, New York

Chicago Museum of Natural History, Chicago

Dumbarton Oaks, Washington, D.C.

Hamburgisches Museum für Völkerkunde, Hamburg

Instituto Nacional de Antropología e Historia, Mexico Museo Nacional de Antropología, Mexico City

Los Angeles County Museum of Natural History, Los Angeles

Metropolitan Museum of Art, New York

Musée de l'Homme, Paris

Museo Arqueología del Estado de Mexico, Tenango

Museo Nazionale Preistorico ed Etnografico Luigi Pigorini, Rome

Museum für Völkerkunde, Basel

Museum für Völkerkunde, Vienna

Museum of the American Indian, Heye Foundation, New York

Museum of Mankind, British Museum, London

Peabody Museum of Archaeology and Ethnology, Harvard University, Cambridge

Philadelphia Museum of Art, Philadelphia

Staatliche Museen Preussischer Kulturbesitz, Museum für Völkerkunde, Berlin

Staatliches Museum für Völkerkunde, Munich

INDEX

Tula

TOLTEC WARRIOR

PYRAMIDS
AT TEOTIHUACAN

Teotihuacan

Tenayuca

*Lake
Tetzcoco*

Tetzcoco

Tlacopan

Tlatelolco

Chapultepec

Tenochtitlan
(Mexico City)

EMBLEM OF
TENOCHTITLAN

Colhuacan

Tlaxcala

GRASSHOPPER

Cuicuilco

La Malinche

Iztaccihuatl

EAGLE KNIGHT

Cholula

Pass of Cortés

Malinalco

Teopanzolco

Cuernavaca

Popocatepetl

Chalcatzingo

0   15   25 miles